I Will Survive

I Will Survive

THE BOOK

Gloria Gaynor

ST. MARTIN'S PRESS ❧ NEW YORK

A previous edition of this book was published under the title *Soul Survivor* by HarperCollins UK in 1995.

All photos courtesy of the author.

Design by Bryanna Millis

Library of Congress Cataloging-in-Publication Data

Gaynor, Gloria.
   I will survive : the book / Gloria Gaynor.
      p.   cm.
   ISBN 0-312-16869-1
   1. Gaynor, Gloria.   2. Singers—United States—Biography.
I. Title.
ML420.G307A3 1997
782.42164'092—dc21
   [B]   97-2591
                                                         CIP
                                                         MN

First Edition: October 1997

10 9 8 7 6 5 4 3 2 1

I can now sing "I am what I am" with true conviction because I allow only the one who made me to define "What I Am."

I can now sing "I Will Survive" with true conviction because my strength to live and assurance that I will comes from submission to the only one who can create life . . . *Jesus Christ*.

CONTENTS

PART FOUR

ACKNOWLEDGMENTS

First and foremost, all praise is to my Lord and Savior Christ Jesus who has opened the door of opportunity for this book, and without whose annointing this book cannot reach its full potential any more than I can. Therefore, I praise and thank Him. For my husband, Linwood, who has always done his best for me, professionally and personally, and whose love is one of God's greatest gifts to me. For my mother, from whom I inherited my humor and mother wit, with which I've written much of this book and the wisdom I carried but had not the courage to walk in, in my earlier years. For Pastor Bernard, who has been my spiritual father, giving so much guidance and instruction to bring about the spiritual maturity that I purpose to share herein. For Pastor Johnson, who has been a wonderful mentor, always just a phone call away. For Fippy, Sondra, Darcel, and Bebe, my best friends, who have invested in our friendship, love, encouragement, time, talent, and treasury, above and beyond the call.

I Will Survive

INTRODUCTION

*W*hen I first sang "I Will Survive," in 1978, I sang it from the heart. I wanted to encourage everybody—including myself—to believe that we could survive. I had had a lot of heartache and suffering, and I thought that I had made it through. What I didn't know then, and so wasn't able to tell anybody else, was *how* to survive, how to get better self-esteem.

It has taken me a very long time since I first sang that song, to learn its lesson for myself. In the end, I have survived, but not through any power of my own. I have survived because after long years of loneliness, and insecurity, and lack of self-esteem, I learned to hand all my burdens over to the Lord, and now I survive in His strength. If early one Sunday morning you were to drive by the church that I now belong to in Brooklyn, you would see hundreds of people on the pavement, standing in line from 6:00 A.M., waiting for the doors to open for the eight-o'clock service. Even if you stayed and watched while they all went in, another line would almost immediately start forming for the ten-o'clock service, and again, from just after ten, for the twelve-o'clock midday service. The church, which is a converted supermarket, holds eleven hundred people, and every seat is taken, and usually there are more in an overflow tent. When I first joined the church five years ago, there were just over five hundred members. Today there are over six thousand, and the number is still rising. Parts of the congregation have moved off and helped to start new, similar churches in other parts of the city. We have outgrown the supermarket and are in the process of building a new church, still in Brooklyn.

It will have a theater playhouse, a hotel for the many people who now come from other parts of the country, a restaurant, an office block, underground parking for five thousand cars, and a ten-thousand-seat sanctuary. We have begun this project with no money and a lot of faith.

In the Old Testament, before the Children of Israel went into battle, they always sent the musicians out first, sounding the trumpets and banging the drums, to rally the troops and strike fear in the enemy. Our pastor Bernard believes in the ministry of music. I'm proud and happy to sing in the choir there, and to be a member of a Christian community in the middle of the poorest part of Brooklyn, that makes a joyful noise unto the Lord and rallies the faithful for Jesus Christ. Above all, I'm blessed to be learning how to live happily and victoriously by seeing life from God's point of view.

—GLORIA GAYNOR
JANUARY 1997

PART ONE

had to have an operation on his eye. When he was about ten or eleven years old, he developed a weak muscle in one of his eyes and had to have surgery, and afterward he lived with my grandmother. She made him go to church with her every Sunday, and she would listen to Christian gospel-music programs all day long on the radio. Exposed to so much of it, Ralph developed a great love for gospel music, which was to influence all our lives later on.

She also took my younger brother, Arthur, and me in once, just for five or six days, when my mother had to go into the hospital to have my baby sister. My memories of that short time I spent with my grandmother are badly clouded by what impressed me as a child. She was *so* different from my mother. When you have a mother who only spanks you when even you know that you deserve it and then you stay with somebody who beats you at every turn—it's difficult to have fond memories. I don't suppose that she really was mean, just rather cantankerous, as part of her defense system. She was cantankerous because she cared, and was afraid for us. We lived in a very tough neighborhood, and I guess, thinking back on it, she probably felt that my mother was too lenient with us, and that while we were with her, she just was not going to tolerate the freedom that my mother gave us, that might get us into trouble.

She can't have been altogether mean, because when we got older and were able to walk the five or six blocks to her house, we used to visit her on our own. Nobody asked us to go, so it must have been pleasant to visit her. It's terrible how I only remember bad things about her. I'm sure we loved my grandmother—even though I can't remember why.

She was a handsome woman, with a strong face, and skin

like black porcelain. When she passed away in 1970, aged seventy-one, she had no more wrinkles than I have now. My mother never had a really loving, affectionate relationship with my grandmother, but they shared a sense of responsibility, a sort of recognition of, as my pastor would call it, "right of ownership." They never moved far apart from each other, they were always there for each other, and in 1970 my mother and grandmother both died—just a month apart. My grandmother died in February, my mother died in March. My mother had been very ill for a long time, and I sometimes think she was just hanging on to get my grandmother safely into heaven before she finally let go of her own grip on life.

my mother knew who her father was, although we children never met him. Like my grandmother, he came from the South. I called him once, in 1970, just after she died. I don't remember now *how* I found that man. I'd never spoken to him, I'd never seen him, but I suppose I must have found out where he lived from my mother's papers. I telephoned him and I asked him if his name was Moore, and if he had ever had a daughter with Fanny Nobles. He spoke with a really slow southern drawl, and said her name: "Yeeah? Uh-huh, hm, hm, Queenie May . . . Yeeah—that is my daughter."

And I said, "Well, she passed away yesterday." I told him she'd been ill for a long time. He didn't say anything, so I gave him my number in case he wanted to get in touch with me later.

He just said, "Uh-huh. I see." And then he hung up. It was bewildering. I thought, well, obviously he hadn't had any con-

8

tact with my mother since she was a baby, so perhaps there wasn't going to be any real grief, but surely it must touch you somewhere inside, to know that you've outlived your daughter. He called me back almost at once and said, "Did you just call me?"

"Yes I did."

"And you said that Queenie May done died?"

"Yeah."

"Well, my, oh my. Well, Ah'm so sorry to hear that."

"Yeah, well—so were we. She was very much loved."

I told him where and when the funeral would be and all of that, and he said, "We-ell, thank you very much for calling to tell me."

"I'm your granddaughter."

"Oh, Ah see! And what is yo' name?"

"My name is Gloria."

"Oh, Gloria, uh-huh, well, thank you very much for callin' me, dahlin'."

He hung up—and I never heard from him again.

$\mathcal{A}$s soon as my mother, Queenie May, was old enough, she got married. She married at sixteen to get out of her mother's house. Probably *because* she had married just to get away, the marriage wasn't very happy and it didn't last very long. Her husband's name was James Proctor, but he was always called Sunny. They had three children, Ronald, Larry, and Ralph. Then she met and fell in love with my father, Daniel Fowles, and together they had three more children, my older brother, Robert, who became a Muslim when he was young and now calls himself Siddiq, myself, and Arthur, my younger brother, who is also now a Muslim. My father and mother had the sweetest, most childlike, or maybe I should say "teenagelike," love affair—holding hands, licking off the same ice-cream cone, going to parties and amusement parks together, strolling in the evening in the sunset. . . . That's the way she described their relationship.

After Sunny Proctor left, my father, Daniel Fowles, moved in, although they never married because Sunny's church wouldn't allow him to divorce her (although that's something I've never really understood, because Sunny himself remarried in that church later). Soon thereafter, Siddiq was born. A few years later my parents were expecting their second child, me, when something strange happened. I'll tell you the story as my mother always told it to me. I know my mother believed it, and because she was my mother, I have always accepted it without question. It wasn't until I started writing this book that I have begun to question it. This is what she told me happened:

One day a woman came to my mother's door and tried to sell her a medallion. She told her that all the men in my father's social club, the Liars' Club, were going to leave their wives and girlfriends. She explained that a young girl had infiltrated the all-male club and had somehow beguiled and seduced all the men, and was using "roots" on them that would cause them to become repelled by and unable to live with their wives. Only the buying of this medallion, this woman said, would undo the power of the roots and prevent the men from leaving their women. (Roots are literally just botanical roots, plant and herb roots, but there are certain people who know how to prepare and use them to help and heal sick people. But some people use them for evil, to make people physically ill, or to poison their minds in some way.)

My mother wasn't at all superstitious and she figured that the woman trying to sell her the medallion was just a con artist. She asked her how much the medallion was, and when she said it would cost a few dollars, my mother laughed and said that my father wasn't worth it. She took the whole thing as a joke. They were happy, she was going to have a baby. How could this woman be telling the truth?

But sure enough, within a few months, all the men in the Liars' Club had left their wives, including my father. All the men except one . . . the one man whose wife had bought a medallion. And according to my mother, my father came to her and told her that he still loved her, and would always love her, but for some reason unbeknownst to him, he was unable to stay with her. And he left.

There are lots of legends and superstitious stories about the magical power of roots, rather like old wives' tales, and like old wives' tales, there's sometimes a grain of truth in them. These stories and legends mainly grew up in the deep South, where both my maternal grandparents came from, and where their original use, healing, was sometimes perverted. Anyone who uses roots to harm another person is doing the Devil's work, but there is nothing spiritual as such about how the roots work. Just as a doctor can give you something to drain the water off your arm, so people can give you roots to make you hold water, and swell up. I know that cocaine can change your personality, make you arrogant, so it's not so difficult for me to believe that somebody could concoct something out of roots to make someone ill, or even to feel repelled by another person.

But to be honest, I now think it is more likely that my mother preferred to believe the roots story, rather than having to accept the pain of thinking that my father had simply deserted her. She always believed that my father loved her, and I never heard her say a word against him, in spite of what he did. My mother believed she had been betrayed by a kind of witchcraft, and received it into her spirit, and perhaps made herself unhappy and ill because of it.

Whatever the reason, when my father abandoned her, my mother was five months pregnant . . . with me. His betrayal so hurt her that she was unable to eat, refused to eat, for several weeks. And that—I believe—deeply affected me. So much of what I have done has been motivated by a lifelong insecurity. When my father left my mother, I suffered trauma because when she refused to eat, I virtually starved in the womb. In later years I found myself with a great fear of hunger, a great fear of loneliness, and a great anxiety about being fatherless. I've been constantly searching for a father, feeling as though there were an aching void inside of me, and seeing my mother's loneliness, having a great fear of loneliness myself.

And yet—he always said he loved her and they did have another child. Although they had separated, my father still came back to see Siddiq and me, and three years later, because they still loved each other, my parents tried to reconcile their relationship and my mother became pregnant, so my brother Arthur was born. By then, though, there just must have been too much water under the bridge, because they didn't stay together for long after that.

Howard Street

2

*T*here was always music in our house.

We all loved music and constantly had the radio going. I would come in for a glass of water and turn the radio on. If I just walked through the room, I would turn the radio on. I had to have music playing all the time. I remember once my mother took a pencil and wrote on the wall: "Gloria has just come into the house and left again without turning on the radio." She said, "This has to be put down for posterity."

Sunny, my mother's first husband, played some kind of an instrument. My father played the ukulele and the guitar, and sang. My brothers all had fine voices and used to sing gospel music—which was one of the effects of my grandmother's influence. My brother Ralph had a beautiful voice, and when he finally came home, after living with my grandmother for several months after his eye operation, where he'd listened to gospel music on the radio day and night, he introduced the sound to my other brothers, who all then developed a taste for gospel music. Ralph, Larry, and Bobby formed a quartet with a friend slept in two sets of bunk beds on either side of what would have been the living room, with an old-fashioned floor-model radio in the middle. In the kitchen sat a chairbed, now known as a futon, which was where Arthur and I slept until two of my older brothers went into the armed forces, and then we moved into the bunk beds. Arthur and I used to talk from sunup to past sundown, he at one end and me at the other of our kitchen chairbed. We would wake up talking and go to sleep talking. It was always a wonder to my mother what on earth we found to talk about. But we could talk about anything and everything: "What are these pot handles made from? Where do they come from? Have you ever seen the factory? . . ." And just go on from there from one subject to another, just talk, talk, talk, talk, talk. My mother used to say, "You know, you don't have to verbalize every single thing that comes to mind!"

The kitchen was the family living room. It was a nice-sized kitchen—I wish I had one that large now. It had a pantry and a potbellied stove, which was later exchanged for a small gas range. There were two big slate sinks, large enough to bathe my brother and me in, at least for the first year or so. There was a dining table that could expand to seat eight—it had a leaf. It was an old wooden table with a metal top and a drawer for flatwear. The kitchen walls and ceiling were partly papered, and partly made of some kind of metal stuff with squares and designs—it was kind of pretty—and the floor was wood, covered with linoleum. My mother always kept the apartment neat and clean, although the building itself wasn't in very good shape.

There was a cellar that we never went into, because it was full of all kinds of garbage that came all the way up to the stairs.

Only the man who came to read the meter went down there. We never, ever went down. We went down in the cellar in the *front* building, 150, which belonged to my aunt, but for some reason or another we children would never go down into the basement in our own house.

*M*y brothers were all comics. I felt at one time that I was living with Bill Cosby and Flip Wilson. Siddiq, then Bobbie, looked like Flip Wilson and told jokes like Bill Cosby, while Arthur had the stature of Bill Cosby but told jokes like Flip Wilson. They were both just naturally comical. So there was a lot of laughter in the family. People would come and visit us and say, "You ought to have your own television show."

Larry and Ronald were clotheshorses. They always dressed in the latest styles. And Ralph did too, eventually. At first Ralph was a slob. He hated to bathe until he was about thirteen or fourteen years old. Then he fell in love with a girl, and she told him that he stank. She really turned him around, and after that, we all had to stand in line and wait for him to come out of the kitchen, where he would be constantly bathing himself in the tin bathtub.

But Ronald and Larry were always very fashion-conscious, and spent all their salaries on clothes. They looked very much alike, and were always being taken for each other when they were young. In later life Ronald used to have big rows with his wife, because on Fridays he'd get paid, and on the way home he'd buy a red shirt—he loved red—and she thought that if he bought a red shirt and got dressed up to go out, he must be going out to get a woman. But he just loved red. He would go to the local pub in his new red shirt and buy a round of drinks for all the regulars. He had a favorite toast that went, "If anybody asks who sponsored this toast, tell them 'fast-talking Proctor from coast to coast.'"

Ronald was about five eight or nine, and was always a nice size, the right size, the size you're meant to be, not fat, not skinny. He had a milk-chocolate complexion, keen features, and the best nose in the family. Larry is heavier, but about the same height as Ronald. He's got big, pretty eyes and long eyelashes, but he has to wear glasses. Ever since he was a tiny little boy, he's had to wear very thick glasses, and they make his eyes look small, so you're always surprised, when he takes his glasses off, by how pretty they are. He has generous lips and a big nose, like my mother's. He's always been a very good dresser, very neat. All of my brothers are or were very neat dressers, except for Siddiq.

Siddiq is not fashion-conscious at all, and he looks as if he isn't fashion-conscious. He's more interested in what he looks like on the inside, which to me is pretty good. Siddiq was my favorite brother, with his round, Flip Wilson face. He was the most intelligent, the most charming, the most loving, the most funny, just the most wonderful person. He had this silly thing he used to do. He'd run into the house, burst through the door, slam the door, and lay his body against it, huffing and puffing and puffing and huffing, and my mother would say, "What's the matter with you?" and he'd say, "The bear! The bear's after me!"

I thought he was absolutely wonderful. I still think he's pretty neat. He's retired now. He pressed new clothes in factories.

Ralph is the only one who was ever distant. And stubborn. He was dark-complexioned, darker than I am. He got fat early on, in around his late twenties, and he stayed fat. He and I are the only ones who really have had any trouble with our weight. Siddiq every now and then would gain weight, but he could lose it again just as quickly.

Siddiq, Arthur, and Ronald were highly intelligent, probably borderline geniuses. Isn't it funny how so often really gifted people never do anything with their intelligence? None of them graduated from high school, although that was mainly for economic reasons. They all left school after getting their GEDs (general equivalency diplomas) and went straight into the armed forces or got other work.

Arthur had the perfect model physique when he was young, but he wasn't the least bit interested. He also had a wonderful voice. For a while he worked with me as tour manager. One night we were in a theater rehearsing, and I went to the back of the theater, out of sight of them all, so I could hear how the band was sounding from the back. And suddenly, from out of nowhere, I heard Arthur singing. I could not believe the voice that was coming out of this man. I stood up in the darkness and I said, "Arthur? Is that really you? I didn't know you could sing like that."

But he's never had any desire to sing in public. While he was working with me, I gave him a spot as emcee. He's got the gift of gab. My mother used to say he could talk the Devil into going to church. He would stand onstage and do a few jokes before the show, and I thought he'd maybe sing a couple of songs before announcing me—but he *never* sang.

I didn't understand for a long time how anybody could

have such a great voice and not want to sing. But now I know that all of our talents were given to glorify God, so there are those people whose voices are meant just for God. Everybody doesn't have to sing on a stage and be celebrated for their talent.

When I started doing a lot of international travel, Arthur didn't want to be away from home so much, so he left me and went to work for Diana Ross, as chauffeur and bodyguard, which he did for fifteen years. These days he's with Mrs. Johnson of Johnson & Johnson, a wonderful lady whom he loves working for.

*M*y mother cooked for people in the neighborhood. She was the neighborhood mother. She was very frugal, but at the same time very generous. If somebody was down and out, if a child was put out by his family, he could always come and she'd find some room to slip him in somewhere, and let him stay. If children were in trouble with their parents, they would come to my mother because they could talk to her. My mother had a way about her that was unique.

So there was always somebody eating with us, always an extra person or two at the dinner table, although many times we didn't have all that much to eat. Well, no, we always had plenty to eat, my mother made sure that we had plenty to eat, and that it tasted good, because she was an excellent cook, but she would sometimes only have a quarter to spend. Then she would go out and buy fifteen cents worth of bacon skins and ten cents worth of beans, and get her spices down and her herbs, and she would make the most delicious pot. People would prefer to stay and eat her hot pot than go home to get their own steak or fried chicken or lobster—they'd prefer to eat her beans and her homemade bread. Her bread was flat, because she didn't put any baking powder in it, and it was just delicious.

It was a happy time. When we were little kids she would make this bread and cut it into animal shapes, and we'd have our little biscuits galloping round the plate, playing games. She'd say, "Just eat. Just enjoy yourself." She wasn't strict in that way. You couldn't waste your food, but she didn't mind us playing. She did teach us etiquette. We didn't have a full set of flatwear, but she told us, when we went to someone else's house to eat, to emulate what the host did.

My mother was five foot four, and she wore size eighteen. She was fat but shapely, with nice legs; very, very fine short hair, with gray like Flash Gordon, just at the top and at the temples; nice big brown eyes; pudgy nose; generous, well-shaped lips; nice full brown face; and tweezed, penciled eyebrows. She was well endowed in the chest . . . like her daughter. Quite hippy . . . like her daughter. Nice legs—I hope like her daughter! But she had smaller feet than I—she only wore a size eight shoe, where I wear a ten. She was the color of toast, or the crust of white bread. She had lots of tiny little moles on her face and in her hairline, which you didn't see unless you got really close. And she was jolly. She was always an "up" kind of person, with rather a laconic, dry kind of wit, which she got from my grandmother, and I think I have it too. She smoked Camel cigarettes for twenty-five years. Ugh! Because she died of lung cancer, I just hate cigarettes altogether. I thought I'd never smoke, but my mother used to have an expression: "The older you get, the dumber you act." I see just what she meant, because I took up smoking when I was twenty-one.

My mother's best friend was my godmother, Aunt Gee. Her real name is Georgiana Wright. Aunt Gee must be about five foot two, and if anything, she's even more round than my mother was. She's well endowed. She's got hair like my mother's, short and fine, and she's another sweet, "mother of the neighborhood" kind of lady. She never had any children of her own, but she adopted a daughter and her second husband's son.

Aunt Gee had two sisters, Aunt Janey and Aunt Emily. They all used to play pinochle for hours together, with my mother—sometimes round the clock. They'd get up, take a shower, have a sandwich, and sit back down at the table and play some more. I've never seen people who could play cards the way they did.

My mother told me about one time when she was "cutting" the game. It means that you've allowed friends to come into your house to play cards, to gamble, and you charge them a percentage of every pot that's won. She was cutting the game, and the police knocked on the door. Someone had snitched. In those days all gambling was illegal in New Jersey. Only the government was allowed to gamble—with the lottery. So the police were in the next room, and they had to walk through another room to get to where they were playing, so my mother just took all the money and swept it into her bosom. She sat down and she said to her chest, "And not one nickel had better move!"

The police came in and said, "What's going on here?"

"Nothing! We're having a nice little friendly game. Do you want to join us?"

My mother told me that she was the only one with a bosom big enough to sweep all the money into. They never noticed.

The ten years we lived in the house in Howard Street between 1950 and 1960 encompassed all my childhood. We were poor but happy, as the saying goes. Children never mind or even know that they are poor, as long as they are loved, which we certainly were.

We moved, when I was a teenager, to an apartment on the fourth floor of 83 Waverly Avenue, Newark, New Jersey, a government development called the Stella Wright Housing Project, and that remained our family home until my mother's death in 1970.

Irma and Coco

3

Unlike the rest of the family, my little sister, Irma, could not carry a tune in a bucket with help. She used to aggravate my mother so. She used to come into the bathroom and try to imitate songs by groups, with this terrible voice, singing all the parts. She'd stand at the front of her pretend stage to do the lead, then jump back two steps to do the background, then forward again until Mamma would say, "Please! Somebody—come and get her out of here!"

After we had been living in Howard Street for a few years, my mother had a brief relationship with a man named Jo Michael, and my little sister, Irma, was born. The relationship was a mistake my mother made in a moment of loneliness. Jo Michael never came to live with us, so we never really knew much about him, except he was nice-looking and apparently intelligent. Things just didn't work out, but Irma came along in the meantime. I thought Irma was my little baby doll, my live baby doll, and I took her everywhere I went.

Before she was born, in spite of our big, happy household of older brothers, I had always been a very lonely child. My brothers always treated me like a baby sister rather than as a friend, and the neighborhood we lived in, in Newark, New Jersey, was a really rough, downtown area, and I didn't find it easy to mix with the other children. I had one best friend, Grear. In those days Grear and I were inseparable. Mamma used to say that if I had a headache, you could give Grear an aspirin and I'd be fine. But after a while she and her family moved away, and I wasn't to see her again for over twenty years.

Of course, I had a few pals. Apart from the Taylor family, who lived next door and upstairs, and were like part of our family, there was Lester Worthy, whose father owned the shoe repair shop across the street, and who used to give us kids old rubber shoe heels to play hopscotch with. They were the best, because they would land and hold the pavement just where you'd aimed them. Then there was Sylvia Bowens, whom most of us were a little afraid of, not just because she was tough, but because she came from a large family, well known for finishing any trouble that anyone dared to start with their family members.

There were Maxine and Polly across the street, teenagers when I was about five or six, and they tried to teach a group of us little kids to smoke. I told them that I thought it was ridiculous to spend money on cigarettes, which would get you into trouble, and then have no money left for potato chips and candy. Vivien Johnson also lived across the street, with a younger brother called Earl.

All the girls liked Earl Johnson. For one thing, he was a good kisser, and for another, he was one of the few guys who would play with us girls. All the tough guys in the neighborhood thought he was gay, but he had all the best girlfriends. We'd play kickball in the yard across the street from my house, which went fenceless from 151 Howard Street all the way down to the Bowen home at 159 Howard Street. One end of this yard sloped, and Earl would start at the top of the hill and run down with his arms stretched out like an airplane, and when he reached the ball, he could kick that ball so far and high, it nearly reached the other end of the yard. We would all want to have him on our team.

I was a tomboy—not surprising with five brothers. I was very, very active, always running, playing hopscotch, jumping rope, roller-skating. We were too poor for Mamma to buy us roller skates, so I only had one skate. Boys used to get a wooden orange crate and take an old-fashioned roller skate, the kind with two wheels at the front and two wheels at the back, separate it, and put two of the wheels on the front of the crate, and two at the back, attached by a long stick. They would use it almost like today's skateboards. They would put another piece of wood like a crossbar on top, and they would do really fancy tricks on this scooter.

That was a boy's toy, but I found one, and I took the two ends of the skate off, got some yarn, and tied the skate back together again, and I learned to skate with this one skate, attached by more yarn to my right foot. I could do such wonderful tricks on this one skate. I would start off pushing with my left foot, and when I was going really fast I could take my foot up, and my body would almost be parallel to the ground, and I could go half a block like that, on the one skate. But when I finally got the money to get two skates, I could never balance myself. My legs would go apart and I would do a split and fall over. It was hilarious.

Although there were all these kids around, they weren't really proper friends. But once Irma came along, it didn't matter to me anymore. I took Irma with me everywhere and showed her off, and she was the one who took up my time. I loved her dearly.

When Irma was five, Coco came along, courting our mother, and by the time Irma was seven years old, Coco was living with us. His real name was Clarence Weaver El—you pronounce it Eel. He had been raised by a Moorish American mother, a religious sect that came originally from North Africa. They wear red hats with the tassel. I think the Moorish Americans are not really accepted by the Moors in Europe, a bit like the Black Muslims who aren't entirely accepted by the Islamic Muslims.

We all treated Coco with great respect because my mother loved him, but there were things I didn't like about him. Because of the way he was raised, he was very strict with us, and my mother often had to take him to one side and say, "Don't raise your voice to the children like that."

We had always been allowed to ask, "Why?" when told to do something, because my mother felt that if they asked, you should always give children a reason for what you told them to do. It's natural to reject what you don't understand. If you explain to them why, you don't have to keep telling them not to do something, because they soon learn good judgment for themselves. But if Coco told us not to do something and we said, "Why?" he would say, "Because I said so." Mamma would say,

"No, no. That's not good enough." He did try to learn from her, but never really did. I don't like being reprimanded. I never did.

Coco was very good with Irma. She had this terrible scalp disease that looked like dandruff, but it was thick and crusty. It looked as if someone had taken cornmeal and sprinkled it in her hair dry, and then wet it, and then let it dry on her scalp. You could actually lift it up like that. And he was so gentle. I could not stand to look at it, and neither could my mother, but Coco sat down with her with a comb and a brush and some oil, and every couple of days he would just lift that stuff off her scalp, and treat it with some medicine that the doctor had given us, until it was gone. Fortunately it didn't affect her permanently, and she always had a thick, healthy head of hair afterward, although she always wore it cut very short.

After I graduated from high school, Irma and I became even closer. She was seven years younger than I, so I always wanted to protect her. I suppose I felt a little like a mother to her, and tried to teach her the things that Mamma had taught me, but as the years went by, the age gap seemed to close up, and we became friends.

Even when she was grown-up, Irma remained tiny, with slim legs, small feet, and keen features. I always felt very protective about Irma, but as she grew older, she wouldn't have it. She was a wild child, and thought I was the most innocent, naive person who had never done a bad thing in her life. In fact, Irma was the one who became quite protective of me.

Coco stayed with us until some time after we moved into the Stella Wright Project in 1960. We all called him Daddy by then, because we accepted him as our stepfather, although they never married and he was a lot younger than she. I don't remember exactly how long they were together, but not long after we moved into the projects, he and my mother broke up. He had become involved with another, younger woman, and my mother made him leave. So she was alone again, and remained alone for the rest of her life.

So now you've met all the members of my family who grew up together in Newark, New Jersey.

Lolo Chopsticks

4

I only have a very vague memory of being baptized when I was about sixteen. Coco wanted to be baptized, and for some reason, I was baptized with him. I know neither one of us was "born again," and I have only the vaguest memory of the whole incident. The only thing I clearly remember is slipping in the pool, or nearly slipping, and thinking, "If I weren't so heavy, this wouldn't be happening."

Being overweight is one of the things I remember from my childhood that has carried all the way through into my adult years.

Up until I was twelve years old, I was very skinny. My classmates used to call me "Stringbean," "Skinny Minny," and their favorite name for me, "Lolo Chopsticks"—even though it made me cry. They loved to call me that and laugh at me. Chopsticks was supposed to describe my legs, which have always been very long and skinny, and Lolo was short for Gloria.

All I ever wanted to do was to grow big and gain weight. I wanted to grow so that I could keep up with my big brothers, who wouldn't let me spend much time with them, as much as

I tried. I always had a huge appetite—in fact, my other nick-name was "Cookie Baby," because I adored cookies. So I was Cookie Baby, just a baby, and I spent a lot of time alone with my mother, eating cookies.

There are stories that were told about me. I don't know if I have an actual memory of it, or if I just remember them telling me, but when I was two years old the house caught fire in the middle of the night, and everybody was getting out, and they came to get me out. I stood with my fingers clamped to the door, refusing to leave, because I'd found two pennies, and I did not want to leave until they promised me I could use my pennies to buy some Tootsie Rolls. I still love Tootsie Rolls.

My mother told me that the first lie I ever told was also when I was about two years old. She'd gone shopping and left me with Aunt Janey. While she was gone, Aunt Janey opened a box of Fig Newtons. She'd eat one and she'd give me one, then she'd eat one and she'd give me one, and we finished the box. When my mother came back, there was a box of cookies sticking up out of her shopping bag. I looked up and saw them, and immediately this terrible little girl said in a pleading, whiny voice, "You know, um, Mommy, Aunt Janey didn't give me none of her cookies."

But I was also very active and I could not go anywhere without hopping and skipping and jumping, so no matter how many cookies I ate, I was always skinny. I remember one day a neighbor called to borrow some soap powder, and my mother sent me round with it for her, and I put it on my shoulder. I was holding it with one hand, and I was hopping and skipping so much that I shook a shower of soap powder into my eye. It

31

was horrible! I think I might have slowed down a little bit after that.

Round about eleven or twelve, little girls start looking at little boys. Boys aren't looking at that age, but girls are definitely looking at the boys, so I started looking at the boys and trying to be cutesy. I stopped hopping and skipping and jumping and behaving like a tomboy. At the same time I was tired of being teased about being skinny, and increased my food intake even more, in a determined effort to gain weight.

With this sudden decrease in activity, and also with puberty coming on, making my metabolism slow down a little bit, it didn't take very long for me to gain a lot of weight. In fact, it all happened very fast, and to begin with, I was happy not to be skinny anymore. But nobody seemed to notice. I kept on eating just as much as I had before, until I was so fat, all I needed was an apple in my mouth to look like they were going to put me on a spit and roast me. It was unbelievable.

Then all at once people started calling me "fat"—and I was so hurt.

I had had a little boyfriend from the time I was six years old. My aunt Janey lived on the second floor of 150 Howard Street, the front building, and she also rented the apartment on the first floor and used it for a dress shop. She had a customer who used to come in, who had a little boy my age, Lamont, and he was my boyfriend as far as I was concerned.

To show you how sudden it was, my putting on all this weight, Lamont went away on holiday, and it must have been six weeks before his mother brought him round to my aunt's shop again. Now, my best friend Grear was fat. She had always

32

been as chubby as I was skinny. When Lamont came back from his holidays, my aunt called me to tell me he was there, and as I came running out of our house, through the hallway, Lamont was standing there, and he looked at me and said, "You can't be Gloria. You must be Grear!"

I was *so* hurt. I don't think I ever got over that.

So now I started the battle of the bulge—aged twelve—and I have been dieting ever since.

I love to eat. My mother fed us very well, so you see, it's all her fault. (I say that jokingly.) But in a way, it often *is* the mother's fault when kids are fat. Because when she goes away, and thinks you're going to be upset, what does she say? "Don't worry, honey, Mommy's going to bring you back some candy." And if you're crying because you've fallen down and scraped your knee, she picks you up and gives you a big chunk of chocolate cake and a glass of milk. She always does that. So when you grow up, that's programmed into you: Whenever I'm hurt, when someone leaves me and I'm feeling lonely, then I deserve to have something really good to eat. So you have cheesecake, chocolate cake or chocolate truffles, and ice cream, and you have all that silly stuff, because you think you need it, to make you feel better. It's a big lie. A tasty, convenient lie, complete with someone else to blame for your woes, but nonetheless, a lie.

I started seriously dieting in the twelfth grade because I didn't want to look fat for graduation. I was very strict and lost a lot of weight. I was looking and feeling good. Then something terrible happened. The guy I was going to the prom with got killed, just before my graduation. A jealous girlfriend killed him in New York—not because of me, I hasten to add. I didn't know him very well, and we certainly weren't close, so I soon got over the grief, but now I didn't have a date. Then my friend Mary told me that her boyfriend, Cardell, would take me, as she wasn't graduating.

My mother had made me a beautiful dress. The background was a pale yellow with a floral pattern. It had a very fitted, broomstick-type skirt, and a peplum on the sides attached to a sash that went around and tied in a bow on the back, and the top was very fitted. It made me look very shapely, especially now I'd lost all this weight, and my legs were really nice, and I had my first pumps, with three-inch-high heels. I was really in style. I thought I looked fantastic.

I got dressed, and I waited. And I waited and waited. Cardell didn't come. I called Mary and said, "Do you know where Cardell is?"

She said, "Yeah."

I said, "Well, where is he?"

She said, "He's here."

"So why is he there?"

"He's with me."

"But I thought he was taking me to the prom."

"I changed my mind."

So I didn't go to the prom.

Anytime I felt lonely, and I was often lonely, anytime I felt left out, I would eat. It wasn't long before all the weight I'd lost for graduation was back on.

I'm not meant to be like this. I'm meant to be slim, like my father. I never wanted to be skinny, and I still don't, but once— oh so many years ago—when I recorded my first album and they told me I was going to be a star, I decided that I'd better try to look like one. I asked my manager to find me a doctor, and he found me a doctor who put me on a ridiculous diet, in which I took an appetite suppressant and a thyroid pill to increase my metabolism. The appetite suppressant made me jittery, so he gave me a little tranquilizer to bring me down, so I was going up and down and sideways all at the same time.

Don't anyone be even slightly tempted to follow this. The diet was: a glass of grapefruit juice for breakfast, a glass of tomato juice for lunch, and a glass of tomato juice for dinner. Period. And I stayed on that diet for eight weeks. The first two weeks I cheated, and I would eat a bit of somebody's sandwich, or I would have a shrimp cocktail, or just some tiny little thing. But after two weeks I found out that if I had anything at all, the diet did not work. If I ate anything—even a mouthful of shrimp cocktail—I would not lose weight. I thought, I'm paying all this money going to this man, I'd better do what he's telling me to do, and that's what I did for six weeks. I got so hungry that I dreamed that I saw fried chicken walking around in the yard. Then I had this dream of this humongous—the size of a room—hamburger. And I remember standing way back down in the yard. This hamburger was at one end of the yard, and I was standing back, because when you get away from things, they get smaller. I thought if I got all the way down the other end of the yard, I could get my mouth open wide enough to get round this hamburger.

The dream was telling me I was starving, but after the

first two weeks, I wasn't hungry anymore. I had a lot of energy. I was working six nights a week, from ten until four in the morning. We were also rehearsing six days a week—for two or three hours in the afternoon. And I was fine. I was great. I slept well at night.

One Sunday morning I wanted to go to church—I had started going to church occasionally by then, but I wasn't very committed, and I hadn't been in ages. I dressed up in my Sunday best, and because I didn't have a full-length mirror, I went down to my girlfriend's house, which had wall-to-wall mirrors in the dining room, to see what I looked like. She said, "Where are you going looking like that?" and I said, "Looking like what? I'm going to church." I pushed passed her to see, and I looked like a little kid playing in her mother's clothes. I couldn't believe how big my clothes were. I'd been wearing size eighteen. The next day I went to the store to get some new clothes, and I tried on a size fourteen, and it was too big. I couldn't believe it. So the first thing I bought was a size twelve pair of hip-hugger pants, and a midriff top, to show off these curves that I had not had since I graduated. This time I kept that weight off. I'd gone down from 188 pounds to 138 pounds in eight weeks. I had to renew my entire wardrobe. The next week I went to Bloomingdale's and spent twenty-five hundred dollars in half an hour, and I kept that weight off for two and a half years.

I am one who has tried every diet that ever was, and I know that *every* diet works, as long as you stick to it. The problem is finding a diet that is suitable to you, and that you can stick to for the rest of your life. In the end, most people gain the weight back not because the diet didn't work but simply because they haven't changed their regular eating habits.

While you are trying to lose weight, you should adopt a way of eating that's not going to make you feel deprived, or bored, and that gives you an incentive. No matter how you manage to lose weight in the first place, the way to keep it off is to adopt five rules, which you do not break:

1. Never eat so much at one time that you feel stuffed full.
2. Never eat between meals.
3. Never eat after eight at night.
4. Make sure you have six to eight glasses of clear water a day.
5. Exercise for half an hour a day, even if it's only walking.

It was 1986, and it was the last time I dieted successfully. My girlfriend Lesley Lynch was getting married to John Sywilok, and I wanted to lose weight for her wedding, so she and I went on a diet together three months before. I was determined that Lesley's maid of honor, who weighed less than 125 pounds, was not going to make me look like a blimp. I weighed 182 pounds, and Lesley weighed 155. Well, Lesley and John both loved sweets, and whenever he would visit her for a romantic evening, they'd sit by the fire or get up on the bed with boxes of chocolate chip cookies and ice cream... and that's what happened to her. Meanwhile, I was losing weight and looking more and more gorgeous every day, and getting more confident about myself. By the time she got mar-

ried, I weighed 155 and Lesley weighed 182. But if you're reading this, Lesley, I promise, you still looked gorgeous.

One of my philosophies of life is that you should never feel
poor because you don't have what somebody else has, or what
somebody else thinks you ought to have. That goes for your
weight and everything else about you. I believe I am slowly
losing weight now, and that I am gradually getting back to the
size at which I really feel comfortable and well. It doesn't matter what people say when I'm feeling self-confident, but if I
know I'm overweight and people say things, it hurts. It really
cuts to the heart.

I wanted a place of peace and solace and protection from
the temptation of appetite. I have found that place in Christ.
As soon as I took it to Him, as soon as I said—and meant—
that I was ready and willing to be freed from the desire for
these things, Christ set me free. It was just as simple as that.
As simple as turning my will over to Him. I simply had to say—
and mean—I want what You want for me in this area. And
immediately the urge, the inclination, the temptation, and even
the slightest desire to eat these things was gone. Whom the
Son sets free is free indeed. I call that a miracle, and I praise
and thank Him for it. Hallelujah!

PART TWO

First Performances

5

All through my young life I wanted to sing, although nobody in my family knew it. I suppose I caught the desire from both my mother and my father. My father was a professional singer, and sang in nightclubs with an act called Step 'n' Fetchit, and Mamma, too, had a beautiful voice. She never sang professionally, but she sang around the house all the time.

You couldn't live for long in our house without singing. My mother sang, my brothers sang, even Irma, with her terrible voice, sang, and I sang—but nobody paid any attention to my singing, or said anything about it, so I never got the feeling that any of them thought I had a good voice.

Although the rest of my family weren't paying too much attention to my efforts to sing at home, I was in the school choir, the girls' glee club, and also the mixed chorus, made up of boys and girls. One term in high school, we were doing the *Messiah*, and I was chosen to sing the aria, with words from Isaiah 7:14: "For behold, a virgin shall conceive, and bear a son, and shall call his name Immanuel, God with us."

I remember the thrill of being part of the performance, and enjoying the music. The words themselves didn't make any special impact on me at the time. I didn't find them particularly significant. And yet I think they must have somehow gotten down into my spirit, because years later, that exact passage of Scripture was to change my whole life around. But that's a story still to come.

A few terms later I was chosen to sing a solo at the school concert. The mixed chorus, the girls' glee club, and the boys' glee club were all singing, but I was the only one doing a solo. I remember backstage beforehand the others were all saying, "Aren't you nervous?" and I said, "Nervous of what?"

"Well, you're going to be out on the stage there by yourself."

"So what?"

"Well, there are a lot of people out there!"

"What's the big deal? I know them all. I've been at school with them for years."

They were all amazed at me for being so cool about it, because to them it did seem a big deal. To everybody but me. Until I walked out onstage.

I walked out there and stood in the elbow of the piano. The teacher played the introduction, I opened my mouth, and nothing came out. I stood there for an eternity—at least a couple of seconds—and then she played through the introduction again. I opened my mouth and still nothing came out. I had looked out into the audience and all I could see was a million eyes, all looking at me. I was frozen, petrified. The teacher waited a few more seconds, hoping that I would compose myself. I closed my eyes and took a deep breath, she played the introduction once again, I pushed with all my might, and finally I started singing the words: "Only make believe . . . couldn't I, couldn't you, couldn't we?"

The words came out, my voice didn't wobble, and my confidence grew as the song went on. I got through it, and I was really good. (I mean just getting through it was really good!) The audience, everybody, including the teacher and myself, were all so relieved. I don't remember the applause, but I must have enjoyed it.

When the show was over the teacher said something I've never forgotten. She said, "Look, let me tell you something. When you walk out on that stage by yourself—the world is your oyster. Everyone wishes it could be them up there, or that they could be you. Everyone wishes they had the nerve to go onstage. *You* are completely and utterly in control. Now. You can either hold on to it, or you can give it up. It's up to you."

I have never had that kind of stage fright again. Every time I went onto a stage in later years, I remembered her words, and my confidence returned. It's not that I walk out onstage thinking, "Everybody's going to love me." It's not that. I walk out onstage feeling just like she said—and even if you don't sound really great, people are impressed that you have the nerve to go out there at all, and if you enjoy yourself out there, they will enjoy themselves too.

I do sometimes get nervous before a show, but it's never because I'm frightened to sing in front of the public. It's only when something is wrong onstage: The band isn't right; somebody's drunk; somebody's missing; or my clothes don't look good. If you snag your stocking at the last moment before walking onstage, no matter how high it is, if somebody in the front starts whispering, you'll *swear* that they've seen the run—that it's gone down to your toes, everyone can see it, it's all they can focus on, and they're all talking about it. I know it's ridiculous, but that's how it feels when you're up there.

Real confidence comes from knowing what you're doing, and knowing that you do it well. It also comes from simply being honest about your talent and doing the best that you can. That's all any of us can expect of ourselves, or of one another. I don't expect my best to be the same every night, and you shouldn't either. My mother used to say, "Even an angel can't do better than his best," and my feeling is that as long as I am doing my very best, then everything is fine. All I ever hope is that you are going to enjoy hearing me sing as much as I am going to enjoy singing for you.

$\mathcal{I}$ remember one performance more than any other, for it was more rewarding than any other. I was at home, after my mother had had surgery on her throat. She had developed a goiter, and after the surgery, she could no longer sing. She would try. She really tried. One day she was trying to sing a beautiful song that I was very familiar with, because I had heard her sing it hundreds of times, called "Lullaby of the Leaves." But that day she couldn't reach the notes at all, and finally she turned to me and said, "Gloria, sing that for me, baby."

And every time I think about it, I get choked up, because I remember thinking, "I didn't know that she knew that I could sing." I didn't think that she had ever paid any attention to me trying to sing . . . and now here she was, asking me to sing a song that I had loved to hear her sing all my life.

So I sang "Lullaby of the Leaves" for her, and she seemed to be loving it, and for me, except for when I have been ministering for the Lord, there has never been a greater audience.

Footsteps

6

My other first "public" performance, other than the one at school, was when I was thirteen years old. I was singing a song by Frankie Lymon—"Why Do Fools Fall in Love?"—lurking under the staircase in the hallway of 150 1/2 Howard Street, and the lady from upstairs was coming down. She leaned over and said, "Oh! I thought that was the radio." That's all she said, but I thought, "That must have sounded good. I really *can* sing." That was my first confirmation that I had a voice that could be pleasing to someone other than myself. That was the first time I thought that perhaps I might be a singer one day.

My mother was a terrific reader. She was always reading novels. In fact, she read almost anything she could get her hands on—newspapers, books, box tops—anything, and because she was so well read, people often thought that she was a college graduate. She made very good use of language, had a large vocabulary, but in fact, she never got past the seventh grade, because my grandmother told her that she had to quit then and go to work to help with the housekeeping. My grandmother hadn't had much formal education, and she didn't see that anyone else needed any more than that either.

My mother, probably because of this, tried to talk us all into staying on at school, graduating at least from high school and going on to college if we could. There was no money for us to go to college, but if we graduated from high school and found part-time work, we might have been able to pay our own way.

When I finally graduated from high school, I only wanted to go to college to please my mother. All through high school I took college preparatory courses so that eventually I could be a teacher—which was what I thought I was probably going to be. In fact, I still sometimes wonder if that isn't what I should have been. I've always been a teacher at heart, always loved children, so I thought that teaching at elementary school would suit me. But although I graduated with honors from high school, I was unable to find the sort of part-time job that would pay enough for my college fees. But by then I knew that college wasn't what I really wanted. All I really wanted to do was sing. My mother was a wise woman. She didn't oppose me, but she knew very well how precarious life could be in show business, because she'd seen my father and the struggles he'd had. She suggested that I go to a technical school and get trained for some other kind of work first, so that I would always have something to fall back on if a singing career didn't work out.

I realized this was a good idea, but I decided that I should try to get into a vocation that I could use even after I became a singer, so that my time would not have been wasted. That summer I decided to go to a beauty school and learn to cut

47

and dress hair. Later I went on to business college, taking secretarial and bookkeeping courses.

During the summer after I graduated, my brother Arthur and I started going out to nightclubs to listen to the music. Apart from the radio, and my brothers' gospel quartet, and my mother singing around the home, nightclubs were the only places where I could hear live music—and music was what I wanted more than anything else in life. So that summer, sometimes with Arthur and sometimes with the girls I met in beauty school, I began to experience the nightclub circuit.

When summer was over I found a job at Bamberger's department store, as a sales auditor. Bamberger's was to be the place I worked at for the longest before my singing career took off. For the first couple of years after leaving school, I had to take several nonsinging jobs to pay the rent, like typing, which I wasn't very good at, as well as working at Bamberger's. I also worked at Canadian Furs as a Comptometer operator, and at a bank on an IBM sorter and whatever the machine was called that put the numbers on the bottom of checks. Each job lasted less than a year, some only a couple of months. I worked at Blue Cross Blue Shield for a few months—which was to be the last nonsinging job that I had to take. But in the meantime, I was aspiring and practicing to sing.

During my first vacation from Bamberger's, I was baby-sitting to help out a girlfriend named Marsha, when I started to hear footsteps in the apartment above me. Someone used to come in every morning at about ten, and walk about upstairs. Remembering the lady who heard me on the stairs in Howard Street, I began to follow the sound of these footsteps, and whenever they stopped, I would stop and sing. I believed that if I could hear them walking, then they could hear me singing. I wasn't interested in applause—I just wanted my singing to be heard. Marsha had no idea who lived upstairs, and I had no idea whether the person was male or female, although I guessed from the sound that it was a man. So I sang to these footsteps, and I did this every day for the four or five days I was there.

And it paid off! A few nights later, my brother Arthur and I went to a movie, and on the way back to the bus stop, we stopped outside a nightclub we knew, called the Cadillac Club. The sign outside said that Eddie McClendon and the Pacesetters were performing there. We'd heard they were good, and decided to look in. While we were sitting at a table with our Cokes, they played a Nancy Wilson song, "Save Your Love for Me," and I sang along with them, just to myself, because I knew the song. Not long after that, the band stopped, and the band leader said that there was a girl in the audience, by the name of Gloria, and perhaps if the audience would applaud, they could get her up to sing a number or two. I looked around and to my amazement, I realized they were all looking at me, and smiling and beckoning.

I got up and went, very frightened, over to the band, up onto the stage. They asked me what I wanted to sing, and since I knew I could sing "Save Your Love for Me" in the key they had been playing it in, I chose that. They played it again, I sang it, and we got lovely applause. Then I crept back to my seat with my brother.

It turned out that the manager of the club was the man whose footsteps I had been serenading for the last few days. He had seen me come into the club, recognized me from his apartment building, and knew my name was Gloria, because one day he'd been coming in and had heard Marsha call out to me. So for the second time in my life, someone had overheard me sing, and confirmed my desire and belief that I could be a singer.

When the band had finished playing the set, they came over and asked me if I would like to work with them. I said I would love to, thinking they meant at some time in the future, or that there would at least be a few weeks of rehearsal for me to learn the ropes. But they meant me to start the very next night.

I was still on vacation from Bamberger's, so I agreed to spend the rest of that time singing with Eddie McClendon and the Pacesetters. I'd had no training, other than the little bit of technique we learned in the girls' glee club at school. But music and singing were in my blood, and I wasn't altogether unprepared. From the age of thirteen I'd been writing, in my junior high school autograph book, the titles of songs that I had learned to sing from the radio. I didn't know the keys of the songs, but I had a list of nearly two-hundred songs that I could sing. I brought this list to the band the next morning, and we found keys for songs that were good both for them and me, and spent the whole day rehearsing. That night, dressed in a party dress I'd had for years but never worn to any party, I began my first professional engagement.

Two weeks later, instead of returning to my job at Bamberger's, I went with the band to Canada, for a two-week tour of clubs and hotels in Ontario. Then we came back to the United States, worked in the New York-New Jersey area for a couple of weeks, and then suddenly there were no more engagements. The band split, and I was unemployed. Bamberger's took me back. But in those few weeks of excitement I had been completely smitten by the bug, the chance to sing to an audience, the life on the road, and above all, the great feeling of belonging to a group.

I worked during the day, and in the evenings I would go out with my brother Arthur to different nightclubs in New Jersey. We had learned a trick or two by then. Arthur would pretend that I was this great singer from out of town, and tell them that if they wanted him to, he thought perhaps he might be able to coax me into singing for them. Don't knock it. People heard me sing, and I got quite a few good engagements that way. I would never have had the nerve to do it without Arthur being there to support me.

When you start to be successful in show business, people always think you made it overnight, when actually you may have gone through years on the chitterlings circuit, being paid so little that you couldn't afford anything better than chitterlings to eat. There were plenty of clubs that would hire you for one night, or two or three nights, and pay you as little as twenty-five dollars for three nights. They took on relatively unknown entertainers, desperate to be seen and heard, which is why they could get away with paying them so little.

I worked for years in these clubs, singing with the house bands. I would go in with my book of two-hundred songs, with the keys that I sang them in, or sometimes we agreed on the keys right there on the spot. I updated my list of songs so it always included the Top 40. The band would choose enough songs to get through the engagement, then we'd go to work. It was wonderful experience. It built character, fortitude, and a sense of confidence that I could do this thing, working at my chosen craft.

By the time I was being hailed as "The Queen of Disco" in the mid-seventies, my publicity machine had swung into action and *voilà!* The perfect life. The reality is that at eighteen I had just embarked on more years than I later cared to remember, of work on the chitterlings circuit.

Chitterlings Circuit

7

When I went back to Bamberger's after leaving Eddie McClendon, I also took on an extra job, using my beauty school training, at Brown's Beauty World Shop, where the manager, Dolores Newkirk, helped me along and got me customers. It was a happy time, and I enjoyed working there very much. The girls and I used to go out together after the shop closed, and on weekends.

I still did occasional singing engagements. I didn't have an agent or artist's manager or anything, just word of mouth. And then I got a break. One night in the early sixties I entered a talent contest at the Blue Mirror Night Club, and won. Another contestant was Dionne Warwick, whose husband was playing drums in the band that played for all of the contestants. Dionne went on before me. She had a wonderful voice, and she sang a lovely song, and everybody thought she was fantastic, but thank goodness, I went on after her.

I wasn't really better than Dionne, but I sang a song that got the club going—and that's what they remembered, that they'd had the most fun with me. I did it on purpose. I thought that the main thing they would remember was having a good time. So I sang a terrific song called "Something's Got a Hold on Me," and they were just boogying down, the whole place was jumping, everyone had a great time, and they all remembered that. So I won the contest.

A singer with a duet called the Soul Brothers, Bill Johnson, saw me there and took me down to the Orbit Lounge, a club in downtown Newark, where he and his brother Sam sang nightly, and introduced me to the manager. He engaged me on the spot, at twenty-five dollars a week for three nights' work, Friday, Saturday, and Sunday nights. (So I still kept the day job!) Goodness, I had such a terrific crush on Bill Johnson, who was lovely . . . but he was never interested in me in that way.

The Orbit Lounge was a smallish club, with a bar in the front and a nightclub in the back. There was a stage for a four- or five-piece band and a singer, and tables and chairs in the back; in the front was an oblong bar and a small kitchen, from which they sold chicken sandwiches and hamburgers, and all sorts of fast foods. My mother once rented that space and sold food out of there for about six months. I overheard her once talking to a customer who was complaining about the price of her hamburgers. She was her usual forthright self, knowing her hamburgers were better than anyone else's and excellent value for the money. I heard her saying, "I didn't hear you complaining about the price of that thimble full of liquor that's going to give you a quart-sized headache!"

The Orbit Lounge was a very popular place because it had good live music in the back, with Bill and Sam, the Soul Brothers. There was also a jukebox with the latest dance music, rhythm and blues music, in the front, so it was jumping seven nights a week. While I was working there, Bill Johnson intro-duced me to Johnny Nash. I auditioned for Johnny Nash's rec-ord company, which was called Josida, a name made up of JOhnny, SIssy, his wife, and DAnny, his brother-in-law, who all ran the record company together. I quit work at both the beauty shop and Bamberger's to record my first song for them, called "She'll Be Sorry." Everyone has forgotten that record except in Britain, where there is always someone, usually a music journalist, who will pop up and say, "I have that record 'She'll Be Sorry.' "

The name Gloria Gaynor came from Johnny Nash. My real name was Gloria Fowles, but Johnny said, "That is *not* a stage name. There's no way you can use that name. Why don't you choose a name that starts with a *G,* so people will call you G.G.? It will stick; it will be like a little affectionate nickname for you."

So I said, "That's a good idea . . . but I don't really know any names that start with a *G.*"

"Well, you know, like Gaynor or—"

"That's good!" And I took it, and I've been Gloria Gaynor ever since. Johnny Nash also encouraged me to start writing my own songs, so I have a lot to thank him for. "She'll Be Sorry" was a minor rhythm and blues chart success, and I traveled, promoting the record for a couple of months, with Johnny Nash and a couple of other acts that were also on the Josida label, the Cowsills, Sam and Bill Johnson, and Johnny Day. Then the record company folded, and the record died. I was out of work again, and came back home.

I knew Bamberger's would take me back, because they liked me there, but I couldn't face them after having left

them twice to "become a star." So I got a job—several jobs—
for between one to four months each. Then I swallowed my
pride and went back to Bamberger's for the third time, after
being terminated at the bank. I had been sent home ill, and
while I was away they changed over to a computer system
and I missed the training day. Really they just needed an excuse to shed some staff, but I'm rather sorry now that I
missed out on learning how to use a computer—it would be
so useful today.

I really didn't like working in day jobs, and I continued
working any singing engagements I could get, and as soon as
the engagements were enough to support me, I would quit my
job. I still didn't have a proper agent, but I met a man by the
name of Paul who became sort of a protector and agent, and
helped me to find gigs. Paul was much older than I, but he was
kind and he could help me, so we started to go out, and he
introduced me to a friend of his, Charlie Langston, who owned
a nightclub called the Front Room Club in Newark. Charlie
offered me a weekend engagement and introduced me to other
club owners, and I was kept busy with singing engagements in
clubs round Newark for quite a while. After a time it became
clear Paul thought he had bought me, body and soul, and was
becoming very possessive and jealous. I didn't care for him in
that way, and I realized it was time to get away from him. I
moved out of the apartment he had found for me, and moved
back home to Mamma.

Then, at one of Charlie Langston's clubs, I met Cleave
Nickerson and the Soul Satisfiers. At that time the group consisted of Cleave on the organ, Al the drummer, who became
my boyfriend, George the guitarist, and Sport on saxophone. I

joined them and we traveled around the New York–New Jersey area, and then we went to a few gigs out of state. Apart from Cleave himself, we were all in our early twenties.

Cleave was a trip. He got us an engagement at the Fireside Inn, at Grand Island, Nebraska, in January of 1969. On the way across the country there were loads and loads of Howard Johnson hotels, with restaurants at the front serving their famous and marvelous Ipswich clams. Howard Johnson's would be a mile down the road, and Cleave could smell it. He would be in a dead sleep, and he'd wake up—"George? George? Is it a Howard Johnson?" (George, the guitarist, was also the driver.) And we had to stop at every one to get him something to eat—every single Howard Johnson across the country. It took us three days and two nights to get there, nonstop, except for Howard Johnson restaurants.

We had gone out there, to the Fireside Inn, for a two-week engagement, but when our time was nearly up, Cleave called the owner of another club in the area and told him that he was the owner of the Fireside Inn, and that he had this really great group from the East Coast working there, and if he wanted to see them before they headed back east, he had better come in pretty soon. The man came, and hired us right away for an engagement at his club. Cleave did that, calling all the different clubs in the Midwest one at a time. So instead of going back after two weeks in January, we continued to do gigs in clubs in the Midwest right through until the following December. That tour was one of the highlights of my prerecording career. The American Midwest is so beautiful, especially in late summer and fall. We worked in Nebraska, North and South Dakota, and Iowa. We visited the Badlands, so called because, although it is extremely beautiful, the terrain is so rocky and treacherous that it is nearly impossible to cross. In summer the mountains seemed to be painted with great stripes of autumn browns and reds and golds. We saw where General Custer made his last stand, and we visited Mount Rushmore.

While we were out there, the saxophone player, Sport, got married and stayed out in the Midwest, replaced by Grover Washington Junior, the now famous and brilliant jazz saxophonist. In those days we all called him "Junior," but I guess I'd call him "sir" now! Then in December, just as we were setting out for home, a storm started up in Denver, Colorado, and followed us all the way back to New York.

I went home for Christmas and New Year, and found my mother was not at all well. She was so addicted to her unfiltered Camel cigarettes that if she was down to one cigarette at bedtime, she would not go to bed. She'd send for another pack, and if all stores were closed, she'd stand on the porch until someone came by smoking, and borrow a cigarette to smoke before she got started in the morning. Mamma once tried Lucky Strike, having been impressed by the commercial's claim that they were "toasted." Her final word on the matter was, "They should have fried them, because toasting hasn't done diddly for the flavor."

As soon as I got home I could see she wasn't at all well. When she had started to feel ill that winter, she had seen the doctor a couple of times, but hadn't got any relief or real explanation of what was wrong. Christmas and New Year were very quiet, and held very little joy for us, although at that time we had no idea, and it never crossed our minds, that this would be our last holiday season with Mamma. She was strong, and

58

as sick as she was, she managed to go and attend to Grandma, who had almost completely lost her sight and had to be given daily insulin shots.

The dark clouds began to gather when Mamma got too sick to go to my grandmother, and I had to take over. I thought giving insulin shots to Grandma would give me a nervous breakdown. In the first week of February 1970, my grandmother passed away.

Two days after my grandmother's funeral, my mother was taken to the hospital. She was diagnosed with lung cancer. I spoke to the doctor, who said, "I don't know what your mother's made of—but they don't make them of that anymore." I asked the doctor if I should stay at home to look after her—I didn't really want to, because there wasn't any money coming into the house for my mother and Irma, and there were bills mounting. He said that it wouldn't do any good; it would just worry her, and he felt that we should not even tell her that she had cancer, because the anxiety would only make her go faster. He did not know how long she had left, because as she had lived as long as she had with only half a good lung left, there was no telling how long she would survive.

So I went back on the road with the Soul Satisfiers. We didn't go far this time, just to Grand Rapids, Michigan, where I received, not long after, on March 1970, a phone call from Irma, to say that my mother had passed away.

Mamma

8

Whenever I would go home throughout my early career, I would open the door, or knock on the door before getting my key and opening up, and her little pudgy self would come running down the corridor, calling, "Oh! I'm so glad you're home! Oh, baby!" and she'd greet me at the door. When she died I just missed her. I didn't know how I would get through the rest of my life. I was too selfish to even think about it perhaps being a blessed release for her.

My mother was sweet. She was really sweet. I used to lie on the bed with her, and her arms were fat, really juicy fat, and I used to lay my head on her juicy, fat arms like a pillow, and watch television. It was lovely.

She had more children than she needed, and she had more unhappy male relationships than any one woman probably ever wants to have. But like so many women, she was searching for love that she didn't get from her mother and couldn't get from her father, because he was never there. I quite understand that, having gone through the same thing myself. She was young and hadn't been taught anything about love, and she was naive and ignorant, so she made mistakes. But she was still a beautiful person. She was always a warm, loving, caring, gifted person, who was sometimes sarcastic to be funny, or as a defense. She never wanted to hurt anybody. She was forthright because she had integrity. She was outspoken. That was just her way. While I grew up being very critical of other people, my mother wasn't critical at all. If I saw something wrong with a person—I mean, if in my opinion it was wrong—that his shoes weren't clean, or she had on too many colors, or her hairstyle was not "in," I would ridicule him or her to someone else. I'm sure that my friends thought, "Yeah, and as soon as I turn my back, she's going to make fun of me too." I was trying to be funny, and was too stupid to realize what they were probably thinking about me.

My mother would only ridicule you to your face, and only after the thing she was teasing you about had passed. For instance, if your hairstyle was terrible, she would not say anything to you or to anybody else. But the next time she saw you, if she thought your hairstyle looked really nice, she would say, "Now! That's nice! That *really* looks good. *That's* the way you should wear it all the time, because the way you had it the other day, honey . . ."

I remember her telling my girlfriend one time, "That lipstick looks so nice on you. You've got lovely lips, and you ought to use a lipstick like that to show them off, because the lipstick you had on the other day, it made your mouth look as if it was bleeding!"

I would say, "Oh, Ma! Good grief!"

"But it's *true!*"

I'll never forget the last time I was at home with her, that last Christmas of sixty-nine. I woke up in the middle of the night, and I looked out my bedroom door, which I had left open so I could hear if she needed me, and I saw her creeping past my bedroom. So I got up and crept up behind her. I whispered to her, "What are you doing?" and she put her finger to her lips and said, "Shhh." So we were both whispering.

I said, "What *is* this?"

"It's my heart."

"What about your heart?"

"Every time I lie down, I get palpitations, and I can't sleep, so I can't lie down. But I thought, if I walk about a bit, and then sneak into the bed, my heart may not know that I'm lying down."

She was too much. She was making a joke even while she was having a heart attack. She began to be really sick, throwing up bile. She also went slightly crazy in the head. She hallucinated. She went into my bedroom—well, normally she never went into my bedroom, because she always said you needed a road map to find your way out—and sat on my bed and started playing with her toes. Then she asked me to get her some rum and Coke, which was what she drank.

I said, "Uh-uh, honey, you don't need no rum and Coke. What's the matter with you?"

She said, "I know you think I'm crazy. I'm crazy like a fox."

So I called the doctor. As soon as he arrived he said that her heart wasn't pumping enough blood to her brain. So he sent for the ambulance. She had had a stroke, insulin poisoning, and pneumonia. But she was in and out of the hospital in six or seven days. That's when the doctor first said, "I don't know what she's made of, but they sure don't make them out of that anymore."

While I was on the road that winter with the Soul Satisfiers in Grand Rapids, I kept in close touch with Irma, calling her every evening. We'd spoken that evening, after I'd done a show and was packing up to leave for the next city the next morning, and Irma said that she'd been to the hospital, and Mom was okay. But at exactly ten past five in the morning, I woke up, and I looked at the clock, and I just started crying and grieving, because I somehow knew she had gone.

Irma woke up at five-ten. Siddiq woke up at five-ten. And Ronald, Mamma's firstborn son, whose birthday was March 5, woke up at five-ten. And my mother died at five-ten.

I was with Al, the Soul Satisfiers' drummer and the band leader on the road when Cleave wasn't there. I was crying, and he said, "What's the matter?"

I just kept crying, "My mother! My mother!" So he held me, and I must have somehow drifted back to sleep.

At seven-thirty my sister called. I picked up the telephone and she just said, "Gloria . . ."

I said, "I know."

I knew.

I got up, dressed and packed, and told the band my mother had passed away and I was going home. They came back to New York later, in the bus we all traveled in. I traveled home alone, by plane. On the plane I just stared out the window, feeling quite numb. I didn't cry.

We lived on the fourth floor of the project in Newark. There were two elevators, an even-floor elevator and an odd-floor elevator, but the even-floor elevator was stuck, so I took the odd-floor elevator, went to the third floor, and walked up the last flight. As I walked up the stairs, it hit me that she wasn't there, and she would never be there again. There would be no one running down the corridor to greet me. I went into the house, and nobody was there.

I had to make all the funeral arrangements. I got together with my girlfriend Marsha (the friend I was baby-sitting for when I sang to the footsteps in the apartment above). Marsha was very sad and cried, because she was one of those whom my mother had consoled and counseled a lot about her marriage.

I'll never forget when Marsha had been thinking of breaking up with her husband, and my mother said to her, "Look, honey, if you're going to leave this man, you'd better make sure that that's really what you want to do. Because when your love-jones comes down on you, you're going to have a problem!" She always listened to my mother, and they talked about everything. A few days later, my mother and I were passing by their house, and we saw Marsha just going in. My mother sang out gaily, "Your love-jones came down!"

When my mother passed away, Marsha was distraught. We went down to the supermarket to do the shopping for after the funeral, and she said, "I'm just going to this other aisle," and she went off, and I came up behind her, and she was crying. She didn't want me to see her crying, probably because she could see I wasn't crying. But although I had cried for a moment when I first went into the house, I didn't cry again until two weeks later.

I functioned very well during the funeral. I didn't break down. I still didn't cry. I've learned now that when something traumatic happens to me, I cope well at the beginning. It hits me later on.

My grandmother had had a beautiful church funeral at her Abysinnian Baptist church, where she'd been a faithful member for so many years, but my mother's funeral was not held in a church, because she did not go to church, and I knew that she would not want to be pretentious. She'd want to be unpretentious right to the end.

They had put a wig on her. She had recently bought a wig, and someone must have given the mortician this wig to put on her. But I knew my mother. She had never worn a wig. She'd only bought this wig just copying me, because I'd started wearing wigs, but I knew she wouldn't want a wig on now. I said, "No. Nobody ever knew her with a wig. She'd want people to see her, and they'd want to see her as they knew her." They took it off, and I did her hair. She didn't look dead. She looked like she was sleeping. And she didn't even feel like she was dead, not stiff, not hard—she felt fleshly.

It was difficult for me to accept that she had died. I was almost trying to make myself cry, because I didn't want people to think I didn't care. I didn't think anyone would understand. My father was there. My sister and all my brothers were there, except Siddiq. Siddiq didn't come because he felt that he couldn't handle it. They had been very close, just as she and I were.

Sunny was there. Coco was there, and lots of her friends, and her best friend, my godmother. After the service I went over to the casket, and I leaned over and I said, "I'm going to make you proud of me." Then I went away, because I was ashamed that I wasn't crying, and I couldn't understand why.

The next morning my sister told me that she and her boy-friend had slept in my mother's bed that night. I was furious. I'd gone to bed and left them in the living room, thinking he was going home. They slept in my mother's bed, and turned the TV on to watch television, and they told me that my mother kept turning the television off. It had scared them half to death, and then he had gone home. I wished she had beaten him all the way. Later I realized that they were just young. My sister needed comforting and wanted to feel closer to my mother. They hadn't meant any disrespect.

In our apartment there was a short hallway, about three feet long, that opened into the living room, and then through the living room was another hallway. The kitchen was the first room off to the right, and my bedroom was the next room to the left, and the next room was the bathroom on the right, and then the boys' bedroom was on the left, and straight ahead was my mother's bedroom. As you looked into the bedroom you only saw the left-hand side, and the rest of the room was behind the door. From the doorway you could see her dresser sticking out, and beyond the dresser, against the wall, you could see a small television set that I had bought for her so that she could watch "Perry Mason." She loved "Perry Mason." And then later on she learned to love "Ironside"—who was also Perry Mason. I mean Raymond Burr. She just adored Raymond Burr. The night after the funeral I dreamed that as I opened the door and looked into the bedroom, I saw her shadow on the wall as if she was sitting up in the bed. She said, "Gloria? Is that you, baby? Come here, honey. I'm not dead!"

And I kept having that dream, night after night. Such a disturbing dream. After two weeks I found myself walking down the street at five o'clock in the morning, looking for a drugstore where I could get some sleeping pills, because I believed that if you took sleeping pills, you wouldn't dream. I became afraid to go to sleep. The other strange thing was that that was the only dream I ever had about *that* apartment. Any other time that I ever dreamed of home, it was always our childhood home, the house on Howard Street.

I think the dream meant that I just didn't want to let her go. That's all. I just didn't want to let her go. After two weeks the dream stopped coming, and at long last I cried.

Well of Loneliness

9

My fondest memory of my childhood has always been of my relationship with my mother. We were always very, very close. She was really my best friend. I looked up to her, I almost idolized her. She was the one who loved me—unconditionally—no matter what I did. I guess she was like that with all of my brothers and my sister, but I really wasn't aware of their relationship with her. I wasn't even consciously aware of *my* relationship with her—it just *was*.

Our mother instilled in us very high morals, but in the form of common sense. She taught us that you did or did not do things not so much because they were right, or wrong, but because it was only common sense to do them, or not to do them. You didn't lie. You didn't cheat. You didn't steal. You didn't do anything that was against the law. Because nothing that you could steal, nothing that you could cheat to get, nothing that you could gain by doing anything against the law was worth your freedom. And she taught us that eventually you always would get caught. Nothing you could do would be hidden forever. Sooner or later you'd get caught, and you'd have to pay. You could learn from bitter experience that it was not worth it, but it was better to realize beforehand—from watching other people, from hearing stories about people who had been in jail, from watching television, listening to the radio, reading books, anything rather than learning from firsthand experience—that crime does not pay. It was only common sense not to commit crimes. This is what she taught us.

There wasn't much talk, that I can remember, about morality. There was more talk about common sense. I don't know, I can't remember, maybe she did teach us things about the Bible. She *read* the Bible. But it seemed to me that she read the Bible as if it were a novel. But the real reason why *I* didn't do wrong as a child was that I loved my mother. I never wanted to hurt her. I never wanted to disappoint her, because she loved me so much. When I would go out in the street to play with my friends, and they would decide they wanted to steal pretzels or pieces of candy or whatever from the store, I would never join in.

When I got a little older, about thirteen or fourteen, the girls and guys would play in the street, and the girls would start running and the guys would chase them, and if they caught a girl they'd get a kiss. I would play too, but when they started to go further with it, I wouldn't continue. The same applied to cigarettes—I didn't want to hurt or disappoint my mother, even if I thought that she would never find out. The things my mother taught me helped me to develop into the person I have become. I saw her as a very strong, morally good woman, raising seven children by herself in a neighborhood where there were lots of prostitutes. My mother was not one, although we were often so poor it would have been the easiest thing in the world for her to have been tempted to make some money that way. But it was totally unthinkable that she could do anything like that.

So I saw her as being physically and morally strong, and I loved that about her. I wanted to be just like her. I wanted to be talented like her. She cooked, she sewed, she sang: I cook, I sew, I sing. I believe that I learned from her, and from my love for her, an ability to protect myself against wrongdoing, even when being persuaded by other people. From the time I was a little girl, I have never bowed to peer pressure to do things that my mother taught me were wrong.

But of course, the other children didn't like me for that, and I really didn't have many friends. There was only Grear. Apart from her, I can count on one hand the friends I had as a child, and even they weren't really good friends. They were buddies, but they would turn on me in a minute. They didn't like the idea that I was the neighborhood "goody-goody."

Their parents all liked me—and I could sometimes win temporary popularity by talking their parents out of punishing them, because I could help them lie, to get out of things. I was always very imaginative, and although our mother taught us not to lie, somehow I learned to be a *great* liar. I could tell you a story so close to the truth that if later you came back to me, you couldn't be quite sure if I had told you a lie or not. Then one day, when I was in my early twenties, I overheard my mother, who didn't know I was in the house, talking to a friend in the kitchen. She was saying, "My children don't ever lie to me. I've told them that I am not the one to lie to. If they get into trouble, I need to know that I can trust them to tell the truth, because *I'm* the one that's going to help them out of it, but if I don't know the truth, I can't help. So my children never lie to me—except once in a while Gloria will make up some fairy story like 'We ran out of gas' when the truth is, she and her boyfriend had been out half the night. She lies kind of out of respect for my house."

And I was standing there listening, thinking, "And all these years, I always thought she believed me!" I look back now and wonder if anybody ever believed what I was saying, or if they knew all along and just thought, "Oh, there she goes again." There are stories that I told for years, and I don't know myself anymore if some of them are true or not. I told them to build myself up. I think most of the time I thought they would have more impact if they were believed to be true—I told them to get attention, to make people laugh, to make myself sound more interesting. I thought I was the most boring person on the planet and that I had to make up stuff, because nobody was ever going to be interested in anything that really happened to me. I felt you could write all the interesting things that had ever happened to me on the head of a pin, and still have room left for the Gettysburg Address. Like most people, I thought I had good reason to lie when I did. I lied to keep the peace, to keep from hurting someone else's feelings, or to keep myself or someone else out of trouble.

Years later, when I became Christian, I saw a Scripture, in Psalm 119, that says, "Deliver me from the way of lying," and I thought, "I don't want to do this anymore." I prayed to the Lord to deliver me from lying. And now I don't lie. For me now honesty is not the best policy—it's the *only* policy. Peace of mind only comes with learning to speak the truth, and it can be done with perfect kindness and compassion.

✦

$\mathcal{I}$ was always the one who would arrive carrying gifts. You know how, if you give a party, or invite people to your home, there is always someone who doesn't think it's enough that you want to see them, they feel they have to hand you a present as they walk through your door? That was me. I always felt the need to give people something, usually expensive presents, trying to make them respect and like me that way. From a very young age I was a people pleaser, and it is only since July of 1996 that I have come to understand why I've been doing it, and have become freed from it. That summer I went to a six-day seminar for a ministry called Living Waters. This ministry is to help people who are emotionally and sexually broken. It is run by a wonderful man, and is for anybody and everybody. It's a wonderfully safe place where you can break down and cry and talk about absolutely anything that troubles you. The seminar was being held for people who wanted to learn more about it because they might want to start a Living Waters ministry in their own home church.

It was such a safe place. We worked together in small groups quite a lot of the time, and many people shared things they had never dared speak about before. I found myself telling my group about my problem—my emotional need to give people presents. I had always been aware of it, and had told this thing many times to different friends and counselors, but I hadn't realized that I had always estranged myself from the situation and was always telling it as though it had happened to someone else. When I was seven years old, it was Christmas. We were extremely poor, so we couldn't give one another

Christmas gifts or have a tree. I wanted Christmas. I saw other people having lots of gifts and a tree. So I rummaged around the house and I found a couple of old ties that I knew my brothers hadn't worn in a long time and had forgotten about, and a couple of old belts. I shined up the buckles and polished the leather, and washed and ironed the ties. I even found an old baby bottle for my sister, who was just an infant, and washed it and put a new nipple on it. Then I did a few chores for the neighbors and earned a few pennies and bought some wrapping paper and ribbon. I wrapped all this stuff up and put all their names on it, and in the middle of the night I got up and laid it all out on the kitchen table. I woke up so excited, and I woke them all up and made them come into the kitchen to show them these gifts, and when they opened them . . . they laughed me to scorn.

When I said those words in the meeting, "They laughed me to scorn," the tears just came. My heart broke all over again. I had never realized until then how brokenhearted I had been that Christmas morning. I'd always told the story before almost as a kind of joke, but now I realized how hurt I had been. My family had rejected my love as not good enough. I mean, I knew that they would recognize those things, but I thought they'd say, "Oh man! I haven't seen this belt in a long time! Man, it looks good!" and try it on and say, "Thanks, sis." Something like that. But they thought it was the most ridiculous thing anybody could possibly do, and I was unbelievably hurt. Ever since, I've been trying to get something good enough. I've been trying to make someone feel my love is worthwhile. All these years I've been trying to make up for that Christmas. Now I'm so free—to give or not give. I'm not trying to prove anything. In the past I've wanted people to say, "Wow! Look what Gloria Gaynor gave me!" But now I know I don't have to do that, because in this ministry they teach you how to open your heart, not to them but to Christ. And he comes in and heals the hurt, repairs your heart and makes you whole; he doesn't mask the symptoms, he cures the problem as only he can. I saw it happen for many people and each case was different.

As a child, I knew that my mother loved me, and when my friends would turn away from me, or when they were going to do something wrong—which seemed to me was all the time—I could always go home to Mamma. But at the same time, I was lonely, and hurt, and afraid of being left out. I wanted to be liked, and I tried to buy friends by giving them gifts.

Sometimes nowadays I look in the mirror, and I really see my mother.

I think she was always lonely, too. Of course, she was happy when we were young and the family was all around. I'm sure that any single mother loves her family, but if you've had children, it's because you've had a relationship with a man, and hoping it would be for life, you gave it your all. It may have gone wrong because you wanted it too much, and tried too hard. So I think my mother was probably always lonely for a loving relationship with a man, a husband to spend her life with.

I know for certain that my mother was lonely after my father left, and then again from the time that she and my stepfather broke up until she passed away. She didn't want to be one of these mothers with "uncles" for her children. You know, this is "Uncle" Ted, this is "Uncle" Bill. . . . She always hoped that one day she would find a good man who would be faithful to her and stay with her, but she never really did. The only ones she had a real relationship with were Sunny, the father of Ronald, Larry, and Ralph; my father, Daniel Fowles, who gave her Siddiq, me, and Arthur; Irma's father, who was only around for a short time and never came to live with us; and Coco. As much as she wanted a life-long marriage, none of them were capable of making that dream come true for her.

By the time Coco left us, my mother was getting very sick. She was always trying to diet, because she was overweight, and she developed heart trouble and her back trouble grew worse, so I spent a lot of time with her instead of going out. When my sister got old enough to go out with her friends, I would often spend the evenings at home with my mother. We would eat peanuts in the shell; we were both "nut nuts" and I still am. Or she would buy peanut butter and graham crackers—one of our favorite snacks—and we always drank coffee. She was an addicted coffee lover and drank two or three pots a day. So I would spend the evenings with her, playing cards, which she loved, or Scrabble, or Monopoly—I could never beat her. She was a gambler from way back, and I could never beat my mother playing anything.

We always maintained this very strong, intimate relationship, but of course, as I grew older, my mother's love was not quite enough. I wanted a boyfriend. In our neighborhood most girls began to be intimate with boys very young, and many girls were pregnant at thirteen or fourteen years old. If you were still a virgin at seventeen, you were definitely weird. I was still a virgin at sixteen, and because of it I couldn't keep a boyfriend.

I was always rather serious, and always wanted to be

loved and respected. They all thought I was so heavy about it, and the word was, "Don't even bother to try to take her to bed. She's not just going to say no, she's going to take you through this long lecture: 'Do you have a job, or any money, or any prospects? And where are we going to do this? You're trying to tell me how much you love and want me, but how much do you respect me if you want to do this in a car, or in the back of somebody's alley someplace where we may get caught and humiliated? You're still going to be a boy when it's all over, but I'm going to be a slut.' "

It was true. I did take them through all of that, and they'd back off saying, "It's okay. Never mind. Sorry I asked," which left me without a boyfriend. Eventually, I did try to keep male friends by becoming sexually active and it still didn't work. I wanted to find a relationship that would carry me throughout my life, because I saw how lonely my mother was, and I never wanted to be that lonely. Once again I started trying to buy them. I would give them jewelry, cologne, gloves, whatever I could afford out of money I was earning from doing odd jobs, baby-sitting, a bit of waitressing in a fish restaurant, running errands. Nothing worked.

The only time I can ever remember my mother saying something that deeply, deeply hurt me was over this. It was a bit later, after I had joined a band and was dating the leader of the band. This band was missing out on engagements due to members who would quit without notice, leaving us without an organist or a sax player or a drummer. The band leader, Eddie, offered to make me part owner of the band if I would help buy an organ and speaker so we wouldn't be dependent on the casual musicians. I agreed, and when my mother found out that I had withdrawn over two hundred dollars from my savings, she asked me, "Who are you buying now?" I was so hurt. She had never said anything like that to me before, and I didn't realize then that that was exactly what I had been doing all along. I thought that she had been unkind to me for the first time in my life. It was only years later, looking back, that I came to realize that she was right. I had always been trying to buy friends.

I had had two abortions by the time I was twenty-one. Neither time was I having a happy, caring relationship with the father. Once, I broke up with my boyfriend after being intimate, and then fell for the "let me help get you through it" line. I didn't really know whom the baby belonged to. I didn't want to marry either one of the guys, and neither one of them wanted to marry me. Abortion was illegal, a dreadful and awful experience in the 1960s. You'd go to some nurse's place and be given an injection, and then you'd go home and soon the pain would start and you were virtually alone. It was horribly painful, but I wasn't really aware of what was happening—I honestly thought it was just blood I was passing, because that's what they said.

For years I carried the guilt of these abortions around with me. I felt that God was punishing me for them. Even after I became a Christian, I still thought that that was why I didn't have any children. In fact, I believed this right up until I was ministered to by a wonderful pastor at a Shabach Christian Fellowship in Los Angeles in 1989. Pastor Johnson helped me to understand that when I accepted Christ as my savior, I was forgiven for all my sins, even the ones for which I couldn't forgive myself. Christ died to pay for all my sins. I was free from all the guilt. I still wish that I had understood what an abortion really is, and not done it.

All the while I was still trying to find somebody who would love me, somebody whom I could love. I tried to hang on, to make the relationships work. I overlooked seeing my boyfriends with other women—pretended I didn't know about it. I became very predictable, very accessible, never went anywhere without my boyfriend knowing where I was and what time I would be back, so I couldn't accidently catch him at anything. I overlooked his standing me up, or not showing up until he was hours late. I was always afraid that if I challenged him, he would leave me.

My boyfriends never gave me anything, and usually the relationships would end by my leaving them, when I realized I was getting nothing back. Well—if you lie down on the ground, people are going to think you're a carpet and walk on you, aren't they? This went on until I was in my late twenties. I felt so unlucky in love, I even began to think that God was calling me to be a nun. Friends would advise me that I was too good to my boyfriends. I would say, "But I've got to be myself. Changing might make a man like me more, but I wouldn't be happy with myself."

Which may be quite true in theory, but what I didn't see was that I was *not* being myself, and I was already unhappy with me. What I also didn't understand was that I was looking for something much more than a boyfriend. I was looking for something to fill an aching hole inside me, a yearning for something that I couldn't even identify. I just didn't realize what was wrong, or know how to fix it.

Back on the Road

10

*A*fter my mother's funeral, I knew I needed to get back to work to take my mind off it. I found that Cleave Nickerson had been ousted from the Soul Satisfiers, even though it had been his band. The others had all got together and got a new organ player called Shelton, and Cleave had left. I never knew why or how all that came about, but I think they wanted to play more up-to-date music than Cleave did.

The group now consisted of Al, the drummer and band leader, Billy McLellan, a guitarist to replace George, who had had family problems and gone home, and Shelton, who played the organ, replacing Cleave Nickerson. Grover Washington Junior had gone even before Cleave left, and had been replaced by Shelton's cousin, Benjamin. Then it was those four. Al, Shelton, Benjamin, and Billy. We began to work together, trying to find gigs around the New York-New Jersey area.

My sister, Irma, and I had had to move out of the projects after Mamma died, because when you live in a government housing development and your family size changes, then your apartment has to change. There was no apartment available for just the two of us in the development, so we had to look outside.

We moved to Lesley Street. By this time I had started going out with Billy McLellan. Al had been my boyfriend, but as always happened, it wasn't really working out. He was being difficult and I was getting tired of it. He threatened that if I quit him, then I would have to quit the band. Billy overheard him. He had seen how nicely I treated Al, and how Al had disrespected and neglected me, and decided that he would like me for himself, so he talked to the other band members, and they all agreed that if Al wanted to throw me out of the band, then they would throw him out. Which is what they did. Billy became the leader of the band and after a while I started dating him.

Al was replaced as drummer by Ron, who used to play at the Apollo, and we called the new group the Unsilent Minority, featuring Miss G.G. All went well for a while, and we had plenty of work around the New York–New Jersey area, but then gradually it became harder to find work, and Shelton and Benjamin went back to Connecticut, where they had come from, while the rest of us were sort of hanging out, waiting to hear about gigs.

Billy and I got offered a job by Johnny "Hammond" Smith, a well-known Hammond organ player, but it meant that the rest of the group couldn't work with us, because he already had a band. He only needed a guitarist and singer. Billy and I went up to Connecticut to get some pieces of equipment that we had left in storage with Shelton and Benjamin. As soon as we arrived I could see that Shelton was feeling full of resentment, smiling with his mouth but not with his eyes.

They had locked up the equipment and wouldn't let us take it. Shelton and Billy started to argue. I had a metal Afro-pick in my pocket, because Afro hair was all the rage at that time. I kept my hand around this pick in my pocket, and sure enough, Shelton swung and hit Billy and sent him sprawling. When he hit Billy, I lost it. I screamed and went for Shelton with my pick. Shelton had a big ring on his finger, and he hit me with it on the forehead. All I remember after that is this big swelling rising on my forehead, and to this day I have a dent there.

Billy and I came back to New York and began to work with Johnny "Hammond" Smith, but after only a very few engagements, Johnny said he didn't want me anymore. He said he didn't need another "star" in his group. When there's a singer out front, it's only natural that people are going to consider that person to be the star. He wanted to be his own star, so he didn't want a front singer.

I went from job to job for a while. Billy and I split up. Irma was living with her boyfriend, so I moved into a smaller apartment on Custer Avenue in Newark on my own. To keep me company I got a dog called Micky. Custer Avenue is near Weequahic Park, where people come from miles around to see the cherry blossoms. Although I used to go into the park every day to walk Micky, I never got to the other side of the park to see the blossoms. Micky would do his business and run around on his own while I sat and read.

Eventually I found regular work at a club called the Wagon Wheel, on Forty-fifth Street in Manhattan, a place with topless go-go dancers. A traveling band had called and asked me to do a one-night stand there with them, and while I was there, the owner, Sol, asked me if I would like to work with the Radio, the group that performed there every night, playing Top 40 radio music.

Irma was working at the club as a hat-check girl, and she told me that it was a great place to be, because all the producers, writers, arrangers, and record-company people from the surrounding area were in all the time—probably because of the topless dancers. So I agreed to stay there and sing nightly with the Radio.

Sometime between late 1971 and early 1972, I met my first manager, Benny (our nickname for him), who came to see me at the Wagon Wheel. Benny introduced me to Paul Leka, from Columbia Records, who became interested in recording me. My days on the chitterlings circuit were coming to an end. The seventies, the dazzling decade of disco, was beginning, and I wasn't *never* going to say good-bye.

Benny

11

There's no doubt that in the beginning I owed a lot to Benny. He got me off the chitterlings circuit, and when he first became my manager, he was kind and helpful. I became very attached to him. When I first met him he didn't have an office or even an apartment in New York. He was living in a hotel, and he used to meet young artists like myself, whom he wanted to sign up, in cafés and restaurants. I soon realized he could be a bit arrogant, especially in public. We'd sit for hours, talking and taking up a table but only drinking coffee, until eventually we'd be asked to leave. He always kicked up an almighty row and swore fearfully whenever this happened, but it happened so often, he must have known it was coming. But we young artists were impressed by his audacity, and found him comical rather than offensive.

Benny and I quickly became friends. I had lost my mother a little over a year before I met him, and I'd been alone for a long time. I had never been so alone before. I'd grown up in a big family, and now my brothers and sister had all married and moved away from home. When I was on tour, singing with different groups on the road, it hadn't been so bad because the band leader had also been my boyfriend, so I always had someone with me. (I wasn't quite as promiscuous as this makes me sound—I only traveled with three different groups over a five-year period.) And when there was no work, I could always go home to Mamma.

Benny introduced me to Norbury Walters, who became my agent and hooked me up with a white band called City Life, whose leader was Billy Civitella, who was never my boyfriend, I hasten to add. There was Billy on drums, Tony Tarsia on Bass, Clay, lead guitar, Sal, rhythm guitar, and Gloria Gaynor, singer. We were billed as "City Life with G.G."

I traveled up and down the East Coast with City Life, and a year later, when we were getting even better known, we were joined by a singing group, the Simon Sisters, Sondra, Cynthia, and Tera Simon, who had been working as a singing trio on their own with their brother, Linwood Simon, managing them. They agreed to join City Life and me as a backing group, and I renamed them Simon Said, after the little children's game, *Simon said do this . . . Simon said do that . . .* in which everyone has to copy the leader. Benny fell in love with Sondra Simon, the eldest sister, and he started managing their affairs along with mine.

We were on the road a lot, and I positively hated to come home. Even though I was still quite lonely, I had decided that I wasn't going to have any more of these stupid boyfriends. I had come to a point in my life when I felt that I'd had enough of silly men who didn't want to do anything, who had no sense of a future, no sense of who they wanted to be, no commitment to anything, no ambition. I'd just had enough. One thing I had done after my mother died was to sit down and assess myself as honestly as I could. I wrote down a list of my attributes, as I saw them, and a list of my faults. I compared these lists and I decided that this was a perfectly nice person, and there was no reason why she should have to settle for just any man who came along. She should have the kind of man she wanted. Then I wrote a list of the attributes that I wanted in a man, and a list of all the faults that I thought I could accept, realizing that everyone has faults, and it would be best to have a man with the kind of faults that I could live with. Then I began to pray over those lists and asked God to send me the sort of man I'd described in my lists if He thought he'd be good for me. I say that I prayed, and I did, but my prayers in those days consisted mainly of a list of requests to God. I had begun to discover an embryonic faith, but I had yet to come to know the Lord. Having made my lists, I stopped dating.

The band would keep introducing fellows to me, and I'd go, "Pff! Na! Next!" And they'd say, "Gloria, you're not giving them a chance." And I'd say, "They don't deserve a chance! That's not what I'm looking for. I don't need it." And this went on for two of the loneliest years of my life.

I left my apartment on Custer Avenue, Newark, and moved to Manhattan, into the same building where Benny now lived and had his office. We were good and Norby kept us working a lot, but even then, when I did come home, I usually slept on the floor in Benny's office, on a mattress from a rollaway bed he kept standing behind the thick curtains in his office. I didn't want to go into my own empty apartment. I had Benny and Norby book me as constantly as possible, because I never wanted to be at home. Although my personal life was pathetic, my career was really beginning to take off. It was 1972 and 1973, the early days of the disco era, and we were fast becoming big stars.

Benny took care of all the money. Everybody got a salary, including me, but my understanding was that it was my money. My band and my singers got paid, and Benny was a form of protection for me, to keep people from begging me out of all my money—I was a soft touch—and to keep me from overspending. I trusted him absolutely. I never paid proper attention to the balance of my books. Money wasn't important. As long as it was there for me to spend, okay, and when it ran out, okay, I'd go out and make some more. I think a lot of newly successful artists have that attitude. So stupid.

Between 1972 and 1975, we all traveled around the East Coast together, City Life, Simon Said, and I, and often Benny would come along too. We were working really hard, and this was the time when I had begun to think that if I was going to be a star, I had better look like one, and had lost a great deal of weight. So I was dieting and disco dancing, and performing and recording, and looking really good.

Working so much together, Sondra, Cynthia, Tera Simon, and I became really good friends, so after a while we began to show each other our family photos. I was looking through their album and I saw a photograph of their brother, Linwood, who used to manage them. As soon as I saw his picture, I said, "That's the one."

Sondra said, "The one what?"

"The one I'm going to marry."

"Oh! Right!"

"I'm serious. When is his birthday?" I was never really into astrology, but I did know about the signs, and some of the qualities attributed to people of each sign. It turned out that he was born April 18, which was on the cusp of Aries and Taurus, which was quite significant to me, because my mother, who was my first best friend, was Taurus, and Benny, my other best friend, was Aries, so I thought, "Perfect. This is the one."

This was in 1974, but we weren't destined to meet until 1975, by which time, largely thanks to Benny and Norbury, I was no longer a hungry singer on the chitterling circuit, but the recording star Gloria Gaynor, soon to be crowned the new Queen of Disco.

Disco Queen

12

*I*n terms of worldly success, the seventies was *my* decade. New York City became the center of the musical universe, the capital of nightlife, with a host of new stars, and I was right up there, shining among them.

Paul Leka, whom I had met through Benny at the Wagon Wheel, introduced me to Clive Davis, president of Columbia Records, who expressed an interest in making me a recording artist. I had started touring with City Life, but this was still in the very early days, before Simon Said had joined us. Clive Davis decided to record me, but not, unfortunately, with City Life. It made things a bit difficult between me and the band, who kept saying things like, "If it wasn't for us, she wouldn't have got anywhere," which hurt. It wasn't my fault and there was nothing I could do. I signed a contract with Columbia, and I was introduced to Mervyn and Melvin Steel, who wrote my first hit single, "Honey Bee."

When "Honey Bee" was released, it became known as the Disco National Anthem, because it received so much disco play. City Life and I played "Honey Bee" wherever we went, and the song became hugely popular in all the clubs. All the disco fans loved dancing to it, but unfortunately it didn't get much radio play, which really worked against it. The fans heard it all the time in the clubs, so they didn't need to go and buy the record. It was finally pushed on the radio, but by that time it was so widespread and well known in the clubs that it just never reached its full potential, considering how popular it really was.

We were very busy. Norbury got us a lot of bookings, and this was the most consistent work I'd had since I first began singing. We were working all up and down the East Coast, Florida, North and South Carolina, New York, New Jersey, Maryland, and Washington.

We often went to a club in Scarsdale called Fudgy's. Fudgy, the club owner, was very keen on making sure his clientele liked the band he hired for the week. If the club didn't like a new band the first night, they'd be replaced by a band he knew they did like on the second night. Visiting bands were often replaced on the second night by City Life, featuring G.G.

Fudgy's was quite a club. On the weekends the floor would be so crowded with people dancing, or just standing and talking, I used to marvel at how the waitresses could serve them all, and never seem to lose a payment, a drink, or a customer. But one night they did lose one. A man got shot at Fudgy's. We were onstage and saw the whole thing. It seemed to happen in slow motion, and this guy appeared to be lifted by invisible hands out of his chair, up and over the back. The glasses, table, and chair all went in different directions and people moved away as he landed sprawled out flat on the floor under another table. The man who did it slipped quietly out through the crowd. I caught a glimpse of the back of him, but it had all happened so fast, we wondered if it had really happened at all. We were never questioned about it, and I can't even remember now what the papers said it had all been about.

We had an adventure of our own after a show at another club near Fudgy's. As usual it had gone really well, and Billy and I had gone outside to sit in our van parked out back, to listen to the recording we'd made of it. Tony, the bass player, was still in the club, just milling around, and a girl came up to say how much she'd enjoyed the show. Then a huge guy came up, pushed Tony, and said, "Why are you talking to my girl? Come outside. I want to talk to you." Now, this man was really big; he must have weighed over 300 pounds, while Tony weighed 140 pounds soaking wet. Tony tried to explain that he hadn't really been talking to the girl, but this man wasn't having it, and insisted they go outside.

I looked up and noticed two men standing, arguing under the streetlamp. Then the very big man punched the little man, who went down like a sack of potatoes, and by the light of the streetlamp on his face, I saw it was Tony. I jumped out of the van and ran up and punched the man. Tony jumped up and ran off down the road. The man ignored me completely and took off after Tony. I ran after him, calling out, "Don't go down there alone, Tony. Come back this way."

Tony heard me, veered around a parked car, and started running back toward me, but he stumbled and fell over his platform shoes. The fat man pounced on top of him. Billy and I both jumped on top of the man to try to pull him off Tony, and we were joined by Clay. It took all three of us to get him off. Clay took off with Tony and they both ran around to the front door of the club, but it wouldn't open. So they ran back around the back door, with this man on their heels, and Billy and I, who hadn't been able to hold him, hotly pursuing him. As we drew near we saw Tony running toward the stairs up to the club door, and I screamed, "No! Tony, the door might be locked—run around the van."

So he started running around and around the van, the man still chasing him. I ran up the stairs to check the door, with Billy close behind me. I got the door open and Billy and I stood aside to let Tony through. Billy tried to hold the man, who easily tossed him out of the way by throwing him over the side of the stairs. He knocked me aside and charged in after Tony.

We ran in after him to see if we could stop him from killing Tony, but although he rampaged through the club, he couldn't find him. At last the club bouncers came along and got him out. When he was gone, Tony came crawling out from under a table where four or five girls were sitting.

While we all sat panting in the dressing room, trying to get our breath back and finding out what on earth Tony had done to make this man so mad, one of the bouncers came back and said the police were outside and wanted to talk to Tony. We all went to the door. Billy and Clay led the way, then Tony followed, just ahead of me. The big man had got an even bigger friend with him outside now, and right in front of the door, the police were a few yards away. As soon as Tony appeared, the fat man became like a giant monster trying to get him, so Tony ran back in and I slammed the door. He was yelling through the door, "Come out and fight like a man!" I was dancing up and down, screaming, "Fight like a man? He doesn't even know what you're fighting about!" He said to me, "Who the hell are you? You're kind are not even supposed to be here." By which he meant I was black. The band was white, the whole town was white, but I was black. I didn't care anymore that he was a 300-pound gorilla and I was at my slimmest, weighing no more than 130 pounds. I was mad. I put my fists up and lunged at him, shouting, "If you don't like me being here, try and put me out!" He lunged at me but because he was drunk and off balance I was easily able to shove him aside and he fell into the hedges. The others laughed and started calling him Muhammed Ali.

He was drunk, and just a town bully. The police came up and grabbed him and his friend. But they advised us to get out of town. They said, "We can't hold them, and you can bet they'll come back—with guns."

We gathered up all our gear, and as we took off in the van, nursing Tony's bruises, I said, "If I ever make a movie of my life, this has got to be in it."

Shortly after the release of "Honey Bee," City Life and I were once again booked to work at Fudgy's. They always had free admission, and no drink minimum. We usually performed nightly from 10 P.M. until 4:00 A.M., forty minutes onstage and twenty minutes off. However, the night we were engaged after "Honey Bee" had been released, we were billed as "City Life, featuring Columbia recording artist Gloria Gaynor, singing her hit song "Honey Bee." One-hour show, $13 cover charge."

I thought, "Good grief, this place is usually full on a Saturday night, but tonight it's going to be empty. There's no way these people are going to pay thirteen dollars to see an act performed for one hour that they've been seeing performed six hours a night—free—for the past two years."

Well, I was never more surprised or flattered in my life, and I've never felt more loved by any audience. The place had a legal capacity of 187, but there were over 700 people there that night. We put together a good show, with lots of new songs, and they treated us like real stars. I signed my first autograph that night. The young man who asked for it and I were both shaking like leaves. I shall never forget it.

*I*n the east we were getting a better and better reception everywhere we went. We were playing most of the Top 40 tunes, and "Honey Bee," of course, being my record, was one. We had also started including in our set a new arrangement of a song that I had been singing in a rhythm and blues arrangement with the Unsilent Majority, even before I joined up with City Life. The song was "Never Can Say Goodbye," and we made a sort of cross between the Isaac Hayes version and the Jackson Five hit, a funky disco version. We were having even more success with this in the clubs than with "Honey Bee."

Meanwhile, Clive Davis had left Columbia Records and moved to another label. I still had my contract with Columbia, but somehow the people who took over Clive Davis's position were not interested in the projects that he'd brought in, and I kind of got lost in the shuffle.

Then, still in 1972, Bruce Greenberg from MGM records heard "Honey Bee" and decided he wanted the record and the artist. He contacted Columbia, which agreed to release me. They told him to deal with Benny, who worked out the buying out of my contract from Columbia, but it was very nearly a fiasco. There were endless delays and disagreements about the contract. In the end MGM telephoned at five-thirty on Friday afternoon to say that if it didn't have the signed contract by 6:00 P.M. that day, the deal was off. I had to go by foot down to their offices with the signed contract, running all the way from Eighth and Fifty-fifth Street to Fifty-second and Sixth, and back to Seventh, in exactly half an hour. In Manhattan in the rush hour, it would have taken me three times longer by cab.

I invited Bruce Greenberg and the MGM president down to hear us perform "Never Can Say Goodbye," because I was convinced that it should be my next single. I told them that "Honey Bee" had become a sort of cult hit in the discos, but that we were getting as much, if not more, response with our disco version of "Never Can Say Goodbye." They saw that I was right. We did it, and it was a big, worldwide seller. I continued traveling with City Life and Simon Said, but once again my recording career caused problems with City Life. "Never Can Say Goodbye" was a song that we had been playing together in the clubs, and it was their arrangement. Bruce Greenberg of MGM liked the arrangement, but when it came to making the recording, he gave it to his studio arranger to sort out, and of course, he wanted to make it for a larger band. Studio orchestras are usually about thirty-five or forty pieces. He didn't alter the arrangement, he just wrote in more parts. I insisted that the band be allowed to play on the recording, and be given credit for their arrangement, but they had had no experience at playing in a studio with other musicians, and in fact, they couldn't read music. So when they came into the studio and were given their parts, they thought their arrangement was ruined. The record became a smash hit, and has been a hit ever since, so obviously their arrangement wasn't messed up. But they never understood it, felt betrayed, and I had problems with City Life from then on. It was really just a failure of communication, and such a pity. They did get credit for their arrangement, but our relationship was never really the same after that.

"Never Can Say Goodbye" was the first disco record ever to be played on AM radio—a fact that has even gotten into the *World Book Encyclopedia*. In 1974 MGM released the album called *Never Can Say Goodbye*, with "Honey Bee" as one of the tracks. It was the first album ever to be made of nonstop programmed dance music. It went gold, and I guess it was really a milestone in the new kind of disco music everyone was going for.

Almost immediately after that, MGM merged with Polydor, and for the next few years all my albums came out on the Polydor label. In 1975 we made the album *Experience Gloria Gaynor*, which made the Top 40, and it included a song called "I'm Still Yours." It was the first song I ever wrote, when I was still a teenager, encouraged by Johnny Nash.

I've been a lot of places
I've met a lot of guys
If one did not have curly hair
Then he had pretty eyes.
But I don't know what's wrong with me
I couldn't seem to care
I just could not accept the love

95

I Will Survive

They offered me to share
'Cos I'm still yours.

I never thought you'd haunt me
The way you seem to be
I thought that when you let me go
That I would just be free
But I can't seem to tell my heart
I can't make it understand
There may be someone else for me
You're not the only man
I'm still yours

I'm like a slave whose master says
He no longer reigns
Although you're gone
My heart and my mind are still warded by your chains
If you can't leave my heart alone
And stop toying with my soul
Then please come back
You've got my life to mold, to have, to hold
'Cos I'm still yours

Isn't that dramatic? I still rather like that song.

In the early seventies we became big stars of disco: "City Life, featuring G.G., with Simon Said." The Simon sisters joined us almost immediately after the release of "Never Can Say Goodbye." We were soon earning big money. Disco music was all the rage and everybody wanted us—or nearly everyone. There was one more place we went to that turned out to be a near disaster.

Disco Queen

We were invited to perform at a country and western club in Maryland. It was a small club in a rural area, but known for its really good country and western music. We were the first disco act ever to be asked to come to this club. I don't know why they started with us, because we cost a lot to hire in those days, and we had to travel a long way from New York, and be put up in a hotel, which all costs money. Really they should have started with some local disco act to see how they went over, but they had made a deal with us, and we had come. Unfortunately they hadn't advertised this fact. The regular clientele knew, and stayed away in droves because they only liked country music. But the sort of people who might have liked disco didn't know we were there, so you can imagine that not a lot of people showed up.

The club owner was disappointed, to say the least. When we drove up, he was far from cordial. Actually, he was nasty. We set up our equipment and checked out the dressing rooms—which hadn't been cleaned up for us—and it became very clear that this man had an attitude.

We went off to check into our hotel, and when we came back in the evening for the gig, the manager was in an even fouler mood. Paul Caldwell, our young road manager, came into the dressing room that I was sharing with Simon Said and warned us that we might not be able to go on. He said, "Look, girls, go on getting ready for the show, but be prepared not to perform tonight. This man does not want to pay us. He's telling me that he can't pay us until after the show, and I'm telling him that our contract is for us to be paid before the show, in cash or with a certified check. And he's telling me that not enough people have come in yet, he hasn't collected enough money, and so we'll have to wait. . . . The man obviously does not want to pay."

We had come all the way to Maryland. We wanted to work, and we wanted to be paid. So Paul went back out again to talk to this man, and when he came back he said, "This man wants us to leave. He wants us to leave *now*. He does not want us to go on, and he does not want to pay us. And I'm telling him that he's breaking the contract, and that he has to pay us whether we go on or not, because we're here, ready and willing to go on. He says he doesn't care about any contract. All he knows is that he expected us to draw a lot of people and that we haven't.

"He's even got the police out there. And the police are going to run us out. He's telling the police that we've treated *him* badly! That we've talked nasty to him and threatened him and all that. The police want to come back here and question you. I've told them that you aren't dressed yet. I want you to act like you're scared—like this man has threatened you and scared you." So now we're thinking we've got to be actresses here.

I had this bright idea that when the cops came in, the mascara we had put into our eyes would burn, and our eyes would look red. We would look as if we had been crying. But the mascara didn't work. Unfortunately we had gotten *great* mascara—it didn't burn your eyes! So now our eyes and faces were *black* with all this mascara we'd been putting on, but we didn't look at all upset—in fact, we were laughing hysterically. When we saw the cops at the door, we hid our faces in our arms. We were lying across the table with our heads in our arms, sniggering and laughing, but trying to make it sound as if we were crying. Well, now the police were *really* concerned. What had happened? Had somebody hurt these poor girls? What did the man say? But, of course, we were all the more tickled, and we could not stop laughing. They thought it was hysteria, and said, "Don't worry, sweethearts, the man is not going to hurt you. It's okay. We'll take care of everything."

The cops talked to Paul and told him that the man obviously wasn't going to pay, and they couldn't make him pay, so it was best that we leave and wait to sort everything out with our lawyer when we got back home. We gathered up our things, left the club, and drove back to the hotel.

Simon Said's older sister, Barbara, lived in Maryland and had been intending to come to the show that night. We called her and asked her to come to the hotel and get us so that we— her three sisters and I—could go and have dinner and spend the night with her, leaving Paul and City Life at the hotel with our tour bus.

The next morning, when we got back to the hotel, City Life was standing outside, with their equipment and luggage all loaded on the bus and the police were there. It seems the club owner had called the police again and gotten them to believe that we were all liars. The police weren't a bit friendly, and told us that we had twenty minutes to pack up our things and leave town.

I was furious. I told them, "You can have ten of those minutes back." In less than ten minutes we had gathered our things from our rooms and were on our way out of town. Maryland then was known for being prejudiced against black people, and it was probably worse for us because the band was white, the singers were black, and Paul, the road manager, was white. They probably didn't like the idea of a mixed group working together.

*B*y 1975 I had gone on The Diet I've already told you about, and lost forty-five pounds. I looked and felt much better. It was just in time, too, because in 1975 I was elected "Queen of the Discos" by the International Association of Discoteques Disc Jockeys, and I was crowned in March of 1976 at Club Les Jardins, in New York. It was a terrific, glamorous occasion, and drew so much international press attention that they had to rope off the streets outside to keep back the crowds. I was given the crown and a trophy and flowers, and I was very glad to have Benny and Simon Said and City Life there supporting me, because it was the biggest thing that had ever happened to me in my life. I was also glad that I no longer weighed 183 pounds.

And the press very much wanted to know who the tall, bronzed, handsome stranger was whom I periodically slipped away from the crowds and the cameras to be alone with.

Sometime in 1975 Benny suggested that I incorporate as a way of saving on taxes. I agreed, as usual without asking any questions, because I trusted him absolutely. Benny was my good friend. I knew he sometimes made mistakes, but I trusted him. After the success of *Never Can Say Goodbye*, he put together for me what was termed "The World's Largest Disco" at Madison Square Garden. I was paid four thousand dollars for that show, but it cost me fifty thousand dollars to put the show together. Because it was too big to take anywhere else, it put me in a very, very deep hole.

In 1976 I made the album *I've Got You (Under My Skin)*,

which went Top 40, but it was to be the last album that Benny had anything to do with, because immediately afterward, he and I had a serious falling out. In the meantime, I had met the handsome stranger everyone was so curious about at Club Les Jardins. At long last I had met Simon Said's brother, Linwood Simon.

Linwood
13

*L*inwood is part Ethiopian and part Seminole Indian. Isn't that exotic? The red in him comes out when he gets a tan—in winter he can get a little bit pale for a black man, the tan fades away, but in summer he's positively bronze. The first time I ever saw him dressed in white, I thought, "This is a bronzed *god!*" Even now, whenever he puts on a white suit, I just fall in love all over again. He's got jet black hair that's really fine, with tiny, tiny curls, and when it's wet he gets patches of curls all over his head. He's gorgeous. Six feet tall. I also have to tell you that he has perfect feet. If nothing else is right in this book, he will love my saying that. He says, "I'm sorry, but I must repeat, I have perfect hands and perfect feet." But he really does have nice feet, and he looks good in his shoes and he usually wears absolutely marvelous shoes. He is a clotheshorse, like my brothers, and he loves hats even more than he loves shoes. He is a real *G.Q.* dresser.

Remember, I had first seen his photograph in Sondra's album at the end of 1974 and thought he would be the answer to my prayers, but I didn't get to meet him until the summer of 1975. City Life, Simon Said, and I had an engagement in New Jersey that night. Paul Caldwell and I had gone over to Queens to pick the Simon sisters up from their parents' home, and when we arrived the girls were not ready, so I was sitting in the kitchen waiting for them. First of all their younger brother, Kenny, came in, and we sat and chatted. I'd never met Kenny before either, and I thought he was gorgeous. He was very, very handsome. He said, "I'm coming to see the show tonight. May I take you for breakfast after the show?"

And I said, "Great." So I had a date with Kenny.

The girls still weren't ready, and I was sitting talking to their mother when Linwood came in. Linwood didn't live there. He had come to visit his father, who was ill in bed, and he just walked through saying, "Hi, Mamma!" and his mother waved at him.

Then, as he started up the stairs, his mother said, "Wait a minute. I want you to meet somebody." And he sort of leaned over the banister and she said, "Linwood, this is Gloria Gaynor. Gloria, this is Linwood."

We both said, "Hi," and he went on up the stairs.

It was like recognizing someone I'd known for a long time. I knew at once that he was the man of my dreams, the one I'd been waiting for all this time. I thought, "Aha! I know why he came at this minute. God brought him in here to stop me from going on the date with Kenny." I went and told Sondra, and she said, "Give me a break! It's not as if you and Kenny are getting engaged, you're just going for breakfast."

"I would not date two brothers. There's no way."

"Well, what are you going to do?"

"I don't know. But God brought him in here, and He's going to fix it."

After the girls and I had all left, Kenny's car broke down, and the only person he could find to bring him to the show was Linwood. We did three shows that night, and in between each show we had a half hour break, and the girls and I would come out and sit with our party, which was Benny, Ricky, who was Cynthia's boyfriend, Paul, Kenny, and Linwood. And whenever I went over, whoever was sitting next to Linwood would jump up and say, "Oh, I'm sorry," and give me the seat. And whenever Linwood left the table to dance with one of his sisters (they were playing recorded music in between the shows), whoever was sitting next to me would give him the seat when he came back to the table, as if everyone knew that we belonged with each other. I felt instantly comfortable and at ease with him.

When the last show was over, I accidentally stood on the hem of my skirt and tore it on the stairs. I thought, "I'd better do this right now, or I'll forget until I want to wear it again." So I went back into my dressing room and began to sew up the hem of my skirt. Linwood says that he came to look for me, saw me sewing, and I stole his heart. He wondered how anyone could be so celebrated one moment, and the next moment be so down-to-earth as to sit down and sew up her own hem.

Anyway, he must have been standing there for a few moments, because I heard the security guard telling someone to move along, and Linwood saying, "I'm waiting for Gloria Gaynor." The guard told him to wait outside with everybody else, and he said, "No, no, I'm a friend of hers."

The guard said, "Yeah? How long have you known her?"
And he said, "All my life."

I could hear all this and said to myself, "Oh yes!"

When I returned to the others, he said to me, "I'm driving my sisters home. Do you need a ride?" I lied and said, "Yes," and waved to Paul to go on without me. So Linwood took us all to his mother's home.

Now, Paul had collected me from my home in Manhattan to go east into Queens to pick up the girls, and we had come back through Manhattan to go west into New Jersey for the show. So now, in order to take the girls home, we had to go back through Manhattan, where I lived . . . but I didn't let him know. I let him pass by my home to take the girls home.

So we arrived at their home, and we all went in and chatted for a bit. By now it was two, two-thirty in the morning, and Ricky asked Linwood if he could give him a ride home.

Before Linwood could answer, I jumped up and said, "Well, I think I'm going to make some pancakes. Anybody else want any pancakes? Anybody hungry?" I had never cooked in their house before, I think I'd only ever been there once, but I started looking in the refrigerator, and Sondra and I began to make breakfast.

Linwood said to the other guy, "No, man, I'm going to wait for these pancakes." So we all ate breakfast. Ricky took a taxi home.

Then Kenny asked Linwood to take him home. Until this moment I had completely forgotten Kenny and our date. I mean he was there, and I'd been talking to him as I had been to everyone else, but I just forgot that I was supposed to be going out to breakfast with him that night.

I was determined to keep Linwood there as long as I could—which was why I had started cooking pancakes—but when Kenny asked Linwood for a ride, I knew I couldn't hold him any longer. Linwood said he would take Kenny home— and then he turned to me and asked me if I wanted to ride with them. I could not refuse.

Driving back again from Kenny's house, we were both talking and talking, and we both stopped at the same moment and said together, "Am I talking too much?" And we both said, "No" together. And then there was silence for a few minutes, and then he took my hand.

We were holding hands on the seat between us and driving along, and I realized that he wasn't driving toward Manhattan, so I said, "Where are we going?"

He said, "I have a nightclub. I thought you might like to see it."

I said, "A nightclub? At four o'clock in the morning? It must be closed now."

"Yeah. But it's my club. I'll open it."

So we went to Brooklyn and he opened the club, and we went in. He turned on the disco lights and the music, and poured us two glasses of Harvey's Bristol Cream, and we danced. It was just marvelous. I was in heaven. We danced and then we'd stop and talk, and then dance some more, and talk some more.

After awhile he said, "I guess we'd better leave," so he turned out the lights and the music and closed up the place, and we left the place dark and silent. Again I noticed that we weren't going in the right direction. This time I didn't say anything, I just waited to see what he was going to do. I sat beside him, wondering what would happen, and he drove to the beach at Coney Island, to watch the sunrise.

I thought, "Oh! This is my man. He is too much." He was so handsome, and so regal-looking. Kenny was a nice-looking boy, but Linwood was a man. He danced well, he was a gentleman, very courteous, he spoke really well, and now I found that he was also a romantic. He was absolutely wonderful.

Before we finally parted, when he was driving off, he looked at me and said, "Do you know what?"

"What?"

"I think we're going to be together for the rest of our lives."

I said, "You know what? I think so too."

I let myself into my apartment, and like in the movies, I just fell back against my door and heaved a huge sigh of happiness. I was utterly convinced that at last I had found the man I was going to be with for the rest of my life.

Linwood and Benny
14

Linwood warned me about Benny, but I hadn't taken much notice at first. I cheerfully went on signing whatever Benny stuck under my nose. I had made two more albums for Polydor with Benny, which both made the Top 40, and sometime in 1975, as I briefly described, Benny suggested that I incorporate as a way of saving taxes. I agreed, as usual without asking any questions because I trusted him absolutely.

One day we were all going off on the road for a short tour, and Linwood was taking me in his car while everybody else was going on the bus. Benny came down to the car with some papers for me to sign, I signed them, and he went on back into his office. Linwood said, "What was that?"

I looked at him as if to say, *None of your business,* and asked, "Why?"

He said, "Well, I mean, it was the way you signed them. Do you know what they were?"

I said, "No. I don't know what they were. It's not important."

"What do you mean, it's not important? You just sign stuff, and you don't even know what you are signing?"

"Well, Benny's my friend. He's not going to have me sign anything that's going to hurt me."

"Well, that's probably true, but there is such a thing as conflict of interest. There might be something that is bad for you that's good for him, or if it's good for you, it could be bad for him. He has a lawyer who makes sure that he does what's good for him. You should have one too. And you certainly shouldn't be signing anything without even looking at it."

I said, "Ach, you're right. Okay. No problem. Don't worry about it."

I knew he was right, but I really didn't pay too much attention to it.

By then I had started appearing on television shows, and because of one show, I *nearly* went out on a date with George Foreman. I appeared on "Don Kirschner's Rock Concert," and George Foreman must have been watching, because he sent someone around to ask me if I would go out with him. I had to tell you this, because I think George Foreman is absolutely wonderful. I don't know if he's got five or six sons now, but they are all christened "George." Isn't that great? But anyway, I was in love with Linwood by this time, so I turned George down. There—that shows you how madly in love I was.

Benny realized that Linwood knew about business. He had successfully managed his sisters and he had been a New York Port Authority policeman for about eight years when I first met him. Benny didn't like the idea of Linwood being around. He had never minded my having a boyfriend before, because he knew they were all rubbish. When I started going out with Linwood, his attitude toward me began to change. He was much less friendly.

Once he even tried to frame Linwood. He asked Linwood to go to his office one day and pick up some papers he'd left behind on his desk. Linwood said, "Sure." He took Benny's key and went back into the office block while we all waited outside. Linwood came back out and gave Benny the papers and his key. Later Benny accused Linwood of stealing a few hundred dollars from the office safe. What he didn't know was that when Linwood had gone inside the building, he had run into the company accountant, and he, not Linwood, had gone into the office to pick up Benny's papers for him. So that made Benny even more furious.

As I have said, Benny had drawn up an incorporation document for me. After my conversation with Linwood, and particularly after increasing signs of Benny becoming hostile, I went to Benny and said, "I want to know what this incorporation thing is all about. I don't really understand."

He said, "Why don't you ask the lawyer? You're going to Venezuela in a couple of weeks, and he'll be going with you, so you can ask him then."

So when we went down to Venezuela, I asked the lawyer about it, and he said, "I can't really tell you, because I'm Benny's lawyer, and it would be unethical for me to counsel you."

I said, "I thought you were *our* lawyer."

He said, "I can't counsel both of you, it's a conflict of interest," which was just what Linwood had said. Then he said, "But it is your corporation. I've got your corporate kit, and whenever you want you can come and get it and take it to your own lawyer, and he can explain it."

Linwood was with us on the plane, and I told him what the lawyer had said. He said, "So when we get back to New York, I'll get you a lawyer."

When we got back from Venezuela, Linwood found me a lawyer, and I went back to Benny's lawyer for the corporation kit to take for my own lawyer to explain it to me. When I got back, no sooner had I opened the door of my apartment when the telephone rang. It was Benny.

Now, Benny had never spoken in a derogatory tone to me. I'd heard him use foul language, but never at me. Now he was calling me the most terrible names. "You slimy———, you bring your——— down here right now."

I was thinking, "What on earth is wrong with him?" I went down to his office, and there was a guy whom I knew to be a member of an organized crime family. I don't know if Benny had ever actually told me, but it had been my impression that he was associated in some way with these people. When I saw this guy sitting there, I got scared. Benny continued swearing at me, telling me that he would see me in the gutter. How dare I go to his lawyer and ask him questions about him?

"I never asked him anything about you. I simply got my corporate kit thing, which he told me I was at liberty to do, and that I could take it to somebody to explain to me what it was all about."

"What do you mean, explain it to you? I told you what it was."

I said, "Benny, you didn't. You told me to ask him."

"You lying . . ."

He picked up the telephone and pretended that he was talking to the record company. He said they might as well tear up my contract, because I would never be recording again. I thought it was real. Then he called our agency, or he said he was calling our agency, and told them to cancel all of my contracts, because I would not be honoring any of them.

I was terrified because he was saying all these things in front of this guy, and I thought he'd gotten him there as a threat. So trembling in my boots, I said, "Benny I don't understand what's gotten into you. I've always put my life in your hands and trusted you. All I've done is ask someone to explain to me what we've already agreed. It's not as if I'm refusing to sign anything. I've already signed it. I just want to know what it is that I've signed. I really don't understand what you're so angry about."

He just continued to curse me, but by now I was angry too. It was obvious to me that all this was about money. I said, "Well, if you want a fight, you've got a fight. But do you know something? It's easier to do something when you don't have to do it. I don't have to have money—you do. So I'm going to win this fight."

He demanded that I return the corporate kit, but I said—untruthfully—that I'd already taken it to my own lawyer. And I walked out. I went back to my apartment. As soon as it was time for Linwood to be clocking in at work, I called him and told him what had happened. He told me to call the lawyer, who sent a messenger around to collect the kit. He also told me to put any other papers that I didn't want Benny to get hold of in an envelope and give that to him too, so I did.

That night I called my tour manager, Paul Caldwell. He was a lovely, lovely young man, gay, the youngest member of the group but the most respected. He took care of us on the road, made sure everything went in on time, checked the stage, made sure we had everything we needed. He was on call twenty-four hours a day. He would do anything and everything for us. He was wonderful. I loved him, and he loved me. I told him Benny was furious. He said, "I know. He's called me and said we're not going to Brazil. And he's called the band and the girls and told them they're not going."

I said, "Oh yes, we are going to Brazil. I have that contract. And the people in Brazil have their copy. We are going to Brazil."

Paul told me Benny had locked away all our equipment and stage clothes.

I said, "Those aren't the only clothes we have. Here's what you do. Call the people in Brazil. Tell them I'm having problems with my manager and my equipment has been locked up, but I still want to honor the contract. Give them the specifications and tell them to hire all the equipment we need, and take the cost out of whatever I'm making."

I called the band and told them the same thing. And in the end, we all went, Paul, City Life, Simon Said, and I.

Unfortunately Benny had gotten hold of the girls, and when we got to Brazil, they weren't speaking to me. They were convinced that I was against them. He had told them that I had never wanted them to work with me, and had said they always had to be back near the band, not at the front with me, and that they should wear dark clothing and never be well lit. All of which was totally untrue. When I first knew they were going to work with me, I had said to Benny that the girls were used to working by themselves, they were an act on their own, used to performing and holding the show with no one on the stage but them. To just be in the background wouldn't be acceptable to them. I was excited and glad to have them, because they were very good, but I thought that at least they should open the show with some of their own numbers, ending with their own hit song. They had made an excellent disco version of the song "Smile," with Sondra singing the lead. Benny told them exactly the opposite.

I suspect that Sondra, who was his girlfriend at that time, talked Benny into letting them go with me, but he had probably said, "Well, okay, go, but you just stay away from her." So for days they didn't speak to me, and I could hear them talking to one another about me deliberately loudly, and saying spiteful things. So it was not a happy time.

While we were in Brazil, it was my birthday. So all this must have happened in late August or early September 1976. I was lonely, and because I knew how persuasive Benny could be, I couldn't completely blame them for believing him. They didn't know him as well as I did. Secondly, I didn't want the promoters and record-company people who had come to see us to know that we weren't getting along. So I sent the girls a letter saying that if I had done anything wrong, I hadn't intended to, and that if they felt I had, I thought that after all we'd been through together, I at least deserved an opportunity to defend myself.

Sondra was always the leader, and she told them that they should talk to me, so we got together and talked everything over, and found out that Benny had told us all a bunch of lies.

We had a great birthday celebration, but sadly, and even though I was in love with their brother, we were still never quite as happy and close with each other again. Not long afterward, we split up.

Simon Said went on singing for a year or eighteen months, although not with me. They found Benny out as I had, and one by one they left to get married and gave up singing altogether, which was a pity, because they were excellent. Apart from their own record, "Smile," with Sondra singing the lead, they backed me up on my recording of "I've Got You Under My Skin," which I think is great also.

After Brazil, the lawyer advised me to end my management agreement with Benny. We went through terrible fights about breaking the contract. Benny tried to sue Linwood for five million dollars for contractual interference. I didn't have a contract with Linwood, so that got him nowhere. We didn't even have a verbal agreement. Then he tried to file a suit in the name of Linwood's sisters against Linwood, for contractual interference, for another five million dollars. Finally he tried to sue me again for yet another million dollars, alleging that I had some girls onstage pretending to be Simon Said. He had really lost it.

In the end, in late 1977, after a lot of really nasty legal wrangling, Polydor grew tired of the fight and paid Benny off. I signed a new management contract and began to work with Linwood. I recorded *Glorious* for Polydor, my fourth album in 1977. Then Linwood moved into offices on Park Avenue, and because all the tracks were conceived there, we called the new album *Park Avenue Sounds*, including an excellent arrangement of "After the Loving." It was produced in 1978 by Norman

115

Harris, Ron Ryson, and Alan Felder, and once again, it made the Top 40.

Benny helped me get started, but if it weren't for Linwood, I would not be singing today. I've no doubt in my mind that if I'd had to go it alone during and after that fight, I would have done what Linwood's sisters did, and tried to find somebody to marry. I think Benny's way of operating was always "divide and conquer." He had spent his life feeling, "If I don't get them first, they'll get me." I imagine he's still the same way. When we were young we thought he was wonderful, but in the end I came to realize that it isn't clever to be thrown out of every restaurant in New York, or to fall out with everyone you ever work with.

I discovered too late that Benny had squandered all my money. He had borrowed $850,000 from the record company against my royalties and future royalties. He would go in and say, "I'm planning this big show for Gloria Gaynor and I need a hundred thousand dollars to promote it." They would give him the check and post it against my royalties. When I was with Benny I didn't even know this was going on. As I said, I never paid too much attention to the business side, and because I was getting my salary, like everyone else, I just assumed the royalties were being safely banked for the future. I didn't know that there wasn't anything there above and beyond my salary, and that there was a big hole in my royalties account. Even after Linwood had taken over my affairs, the record company had cross-collaterized, so I was still repaying all the money that Benny had borrowed in my name. It took us years to get straight.

Benny helped me to get started by taking me off the circuit and introducing me to Paul Leka, who helped to get me my first recording contract with Columbia Records. He guided me successfully through my early years as a recording artist. I still pray for him, because once upon a time he was my friend, and I admired and loved him like a brother.

Searching

15

The only thing I can remember liking about going to church as a child was the music, because the one my grandmother belonged to all her life had a very good youth choir. Nevertheless, something more than that must have seeped in somehow, because I seem always to have had a very strong belief in God. God, not Jesus. Even though the services we attended with my grandmother were almost always at Christmas and Easter, for some reason I never got hold of any idea about Jesus or thought anything about Him. But even as a very small child, I used to talk to God, and every night I would say my prayers, and felt He was looking out for me.

When I was a teenager, I read an article in the *National Enquirer* about the earth and the moon, which at some date—I think it was one February 16—were going to collide. The moon was going to come and crash into the earth. Although I did not want to believe it, every night after that it did seem to me that the moon was getting bigger and bigger. I tried to put it out of my mind and not be concerned about it. Then one night I woke up in the middle of the night. On the way to the bathroom I looked through the kitchen window and saw a great, dense fog, very thick and a peculiar red color. I went right up to the kitchen window to look out. The fog was so thick and red that I could not see the ground—and we only lived on the fourth floor. I could not even see the window of the next apartment, which was only inches away from ours. Suddenly I remembered that this was the very date that the *Enquirer* had predicted that the moon would collide with the earth.

It was the middle of the night, or very early in the morning. It must have been a Saturday, because we were all sleeping kind of late. As I started back to bed, I heard a terrible noise, the loudest noise that I had ever heard in all the days of my life. It was just indescribable, and remembering that it was the date that the newspaper had predicted this tragedy was going to happen, I thought, "Yep. It's happening." I believed for sure that at any moment our building was going to crumble down around us, and we were all going to be crushed to death. I thought for a second of going to wake up my mother, brothers, and sister to warn them. But then I thought, "No, why should I wake them up, if we're all going to die? Let them at least die in their sleep."

And I scurried back to bed and lay down, and said a little prayer: "Dear God, please give me peace and quick sleep. When I fall asleep and this building crumbles round us, please take us all to heaven to be with You." And I fell asleep—quite confident that that would happen, because of my strong faith in God.

Of course, when I woke in the morning, the sun was shining, the fog was gone, and at first I had no explanation for any of the terrible sights and sounds I'd heard in the night. Then the radio weather report talked about the fog, and how thick it had been; later in the day I learned that the redness had been caused by the fact that the manager of the bar across the street had forgotten to turn out his neon sign over the door the night before; the terrible noise I had heard was simply the first jet ever to take off from the new Newark International Airport. But my point is that I had had faith enough to fall asleep, knowing that God was going to take me and my family, should we all be killed in this tragedy of the earth colliding with the moon.

I have prayed every night for as long as I can remember, for all of my family and friends, and from a childhood I had a list that I said in the same order every night—God bless this one, God bless that one, from time to time naming some specific thing: This one would need to be healed of some ailment, that one needed to be given money for some bill. Whatever worries or troubles I knew about, I would tell God and ask Him to put it right. I often prayed for good weather, but nearly always for other people's sake rather than my own, and I honestly can't remember a time when God didn't send the weather I'd prayed for, whether it was for snow at Christmas or a sunny day for a picnic.

Until the day my mother died, that was about the extent of my relationship with God. I would give Him my nightly grocery list, and in exchange I tried to be a good and moral person. That was the deal. There was nothing more to it than that. But after she passed away in 1970, I became more and more aware of a great emptiness at the center of my life. I knew I was looking for something, missing something, but I didn't know what it was.

I had this growing yearning to see my father again. It was

strange. I had hardly seen him at all since I was a child. He had tried to keep up a relationship with me, but I didn't want it. I'd gone to his house a few times, until I was about eight or nine years old—my brother Siddiq took me—but I just wasn't interested in having a relationship with him. For one thing, he was living with another woman, and I didn't want to be around her. And they had two Doberman pinschers, and I certainly didn't want to be around them. Like a lot of children, I wasn't interested in someone who didn't live with us, wasn't part of our family, and after a while he had given up and stayed away. But now my mother was gone, I found I had a strong wish to make up with him, and have at least one loving parent in the world.

In addition to wanting to see my father again, I had a growing desire to learn more about religion: I wanted to find somewhere I could belong, some kind of church community, although not necessarily a Christian church. I kept brushing aside my feeling of wanting to find my father for the next several years, but I embarked almost immediately on my search for a deeper, more real faith. I started reading the Bible, particularly the Psalms, and attending church occasionally. At the same time I was looking into different religions: Secular Humanism, Buddhism, Islam, and transcendental meditation. I even tried Hare Krishna and Scientology, but none of it seemed to go along with what the Bible said. And even though I had never been a regular churchgoer, I had somehow always believed that the Bible was real, was right.

My brother Siddiq had become a Muslim by then. There was a period when the Black Muslims came here and, as my pastor puts it so well, Christians appeared to many young men to be a bunch of women and a bunch of wimps. Most churches do have about 75 to 80 percent women members, and the men are often old. So when young black men were feeling so down-trodden, so misunderstood, so underprivileged, Christianity didn't interest them at all. But this new form of Islam, the Black Muslims, gave them a sense of pride, a sense of self-worth, a sense of respect, and a God Who seemed to care about them. They all went for it.

That was what my brother Siddiq was hanging on to when he went through some terrible times in his life, and he feels that was what brought him through. He shared this with Arthur, my younger brother. I think it was mainly because Arthur admired him so much—we all did—that he became a Muslim too, and has stuck with it.

I, too, looked into Islam, but it really wasn't for me, partly because I didn't much like the way they treat women. Also, I just could not accept their image of God. Unlike the men, I wasn't looking for strength, or something to boost my pride and ego. I was searching for love and truth. My feeling is that a lot of people aren't really looking for truth, or to recognize that they are made in the image of God. They are looking for a God that they can make in their own image, one who is going to be there to give them everything they want, without cramping their style.

The rest of my family have all been on their own search for faith. Ronald began to always carry a Bible in his pocket, and became a lay preacher. Larry, who's a darling, and his wife both go to church nearly every Sunday. Ralph used to sing in his church choir, and was often asked to do the solos, because he had a wonderful voice. Siddiq and Arthur are faithful to the mosque, and pray and read the Koran; and Irma—Irma was a lovable wild child who always seemed to be running from the Lord.

It seems that when my mother passed away, we more or less dispersed as a family and didn't have much contact. Siddiq is the only one who really keeps in touch with us all, and we all love him for that. He called me just the other day and said, "Gloria—do you know John, chapter seventeen?"

I said I knew it.

"Verse three?"

I said, "I don't know the whole chapter verbatim, Siddiq. What's verse three?" (I was quickly looking it up while I was talking to him.)

"It says, 'That they might know thee the only true God, and Jesus Christ whom thou hast sent.' So you see it says, 'whom thou has sent.' That means God sent Jesus, so Jesus is not God."

"Yes he is, Siddiq." I will always believe he is with every fiber of my being. Another time he called and said, "You know what—you need to get to know the metaphysical side of Christ."

I said, "Siddiq, I don't even know what that means."

"Well, you see, that's what I'm saying. You need to learn about the metaphysical side of Christ. There's no need to get defensive."

"I'm always going to be defensive when anyone tries to change my religion."

"I'm not trying to change anything. But you are a Christian, right? Well, that's what I'm saying, I know you know the fundamentals, and you should never give that up. You'll always need that. But you should learn the metaphysical side."

I was looking up "metaphysical" in the dictionary meanwhile, trying to think of a suitable retort to what he was saying, so I just listened, and he said, "Because you see, all the religions are coming together now. And there's no hostility—it's going to be like one world religion, and we're all serving one God."

I said, "I know we're all serving one God, Siddiq, but we're not all serving the one true God."

"So who is serving the one true God?"

"I am."

"And who's not serving the one true God?"

"Anyone who does not accept Christ as God is not serving the one true God."

"Well, in that case, I'll hang up."

"Good. Good-bye."

I didn't really mean to get angry with him. It's just I so much want him and Arthur to become Christians, and he wants me to become a Muslim, which, of course, I never will. We love one another very much, in spite of these arguments, and I'm trying now to only talk about the things we have in common.

By 1977 I didn't want to put off finding my father any longer. I decided that I must see him, and with Linwood's encouragement, I went to see him. He was living with his sister, Aunt Hulda. They were both very welcoming, seemed very glad to see me, and we instantly formed a loving relationship. He became close to Linwood, too, and because I was traveling so much, Linwood saw even more of him than I did. He was very charming, gentle, and intelligent, and I felt so sorry that I'd missed out on knowing him for all those years. This time I could say I loved him.

He only lived for another two years. It made those precious two years even more meaningful. His death really grieved me. He had a beautiful funeral, organized by his sister. The minister was Pastor Thomas, the pastor of his own church, whose sons were all members of a then very popular group, the Crown Heights Affair. What a lovely man. I'll never forget that a few people came in after the service had started, and he said, "You're late! But you've got an appointment that you're not going to be late for!"

I was sad, but it was not at all a gloomy funeral—it was a home-going. They celebrated his salvation, his going home to be with the Lord, and they grieved only for the time that they would not be with him. And there were so many women there—all comforting each other. There must have been six or seven of them! A few months later I asked Pastor Thomas to come and perform another ceremony for me.

I remember a story my mother told me about my father. The club he belonged to was called the Liars' Club, because they had competitions in which you won a prize for telling the best, the funniest, lie. The subject this particular time was: Who had had the most frightening experience? When it was his turn, my father told a story about how he was looking for eggs under some chickens in a barn, and the farmer had put his head around the door and shouted, "What you doin' in here, white boy?" He won that round.

I shall always regret not having spent more time with my father. He always weighed 169 pounds from the time he was a teenager. He may have gained five pounds in his later years, because he had a bit of a paunch, but he was still a very slim man on the day he died. Now, why couldn't I have inherited that? I mainly get my looks from my mother, but I do look quite a bit like my father, too. I never heard his singing voice. He told me that he had once gone with my mother to see me singing in a club when I was about eighteen, and that he had been very proud of me. I never knew.

I continued my search for God in different faiths all through the seventies, until early in 1978 when things went *crash! bang! wallop!*

Crash! Bang! Wallop!
16

City Life and I were working at the Beacon Theater along with a male backing group, two singers, and dancers on March 12, 1978. I have always had a pretty fast-moving stage act, involving a lot of dance routines.

We were doing a sort of fast number—I can't even remember what song it was, but it was one in which I danced away from the background singers, and then I turned around, twisted my microphone upside down, and snapped the cable like a whip, making it go back to them. They would grab it and we would have a sort of tug-of-war.

Well, this time they grabbed the cable, but they didn't hold on to it, and I fell. I crashed backward over a monitor at the side of the stage.

We were taping the show, and Linwood was in the control room watching the screens. The camera was focused on the stage, and they could see the band, see me, and see the guys. They saw me sling the mike, and the boys grab for the cable and back up, but when I fell, I was out of the camera frame, and they couldn't see me. And from the expressions on the faces of the band members and the dancers, nobody in the control room knew that anything was in the least bit the matter. They didn't look over at me, or look in any way concerned. They didn't reach out for me. Nothing. The audience reacted. The whole audience stood up and tried to catch me. But these people onstage didn't.

I knew that nobody had tried to catch me or come and get me, but I didn't know that they had been so uncaring until I looked at the tape later. My thought, when I saw it, was that if you're walking down a street and you see a woman on the opposite side falling, simple instinct makes you try to grab her. You reach out even though it's useless. They never moved. I'd only worked with the three dancers for a few months, but I had thought we'd gotten really close. As for City Life—Billy, Tony, Clay, and Sal—I'd worked with them for years. It really hurt me, and still upsets me a little when I think of it.

Well, at the time, I rolled over, jumped up, got back into the frame, and continued dancing, and nobody knew anything about it.

A few days later I woke up in my apartment, and I couldn't move. I couldn't turn over or move anything except my arms. I managed to reach the telephone. I called Linwood and said, "I can't move."

"What do you mean, you can't move?"

"I *can't move.*"

By the time he let himself in—because he had a key to my apartment—I was screaming at the top of my lungs with pain. I don't remember it. He called an ambulance, and they came and got me. The next thing I remember was that I was high—

because they'd given me Valium shots—and hungry! I said, "Did they get me here in time for lunch?"

I stayed in the hospital for two weeks that time, in traction. I felt better, and they sent me home. Then two weeks later the pain came back, and I was once again in screaming agony. I went back into the hospital on April 15, and was there until July 3.

While I was in the hospital, I began to read the Bible far more carefully. I was in a semiprivate room, so there was always someone in with me. One woman who stayed the longest, and was the last one with me, was so impressed by my reading the Bible that she found my number and called me up later to tell me that she'd gone back to church, because of my example. Actually, I think I was still partly doing it for show—but at least I did her some good.

And I did leave the hospital with a renewed faith in God. I was so grateful for my recovery. I felt perhaps I had been allowed to survive for some purpose. I still didn't know anything about Christ, but I felt much stronger in my faith in God. I felt I wanted to encourage people. I wanted to be a better person. I wanted to be more helpful. I wanted to be more encouraging. I wanted to be more as my mother had raised me to be.

The day I came out of the hospital I was supposed to go straight home, but it was the last day of the International Disco Convention in New York. I went home and changed, and then Linwood took me over in a limousine with my wheelchair in the trunk, and they brought me in at the back of the stage in my wheelchair and set me on the dais. Donna Summer was being honored that year. She had had several hits, and when she came on she got a great standing ovation. She thanked them for the applause and said, "But before I continue, I must recognize one person who should be home this evening, because she's just been released today from the hospital after having had spine surgery, but she decided that she just could not *not* be here. . . . Ladies and gentlemen, could we please have a round of applause for the First Lady of Disco—Gloria Gaynor." And then *I* got a standing ovation. That really touched me. I thought she was so sweet, because it was her night, she was the new Queen of Disco, but she was saying, "I'm queen this year, but this is still the First Lady." A very classy lady, I thought.

*L*inwood's and my love affair had begun from the night we met, but the next day after we went to his disco, Linwood had had to tell me that things were not going to be simple. He was living with another girl, and they had a baby daughter. So although we knew we loved each other, we had to be content with a loving friendship. Then, very tragically, their little girl died. It meant that Linwood and Judy no longer had the one thing that had been keeping them together, and they split up.

The day I came out of the hospital, I moved in with Linwood, although even then I didn't approve of living with a lover. After not working for so long, I couldn't afford to keep my own apartment. Linwood had spent a lot of money on my health care, and although he had kept my apartment for me, it was becoming a financial drain, and we didn't know when I'd be able to start earning again. I'd been earning good money, but all of it now was going to paying off the huge debts Benny had incurred in my name, and contrary to what people believed, I wasn't at all well off.

City Life had had to continue on their own, without me. They didn't get another singer, and they themselves gradually broke up as a group, one at a time going off to join other people. We'd had our ups and downs over the year, but I've seen Billy and Tony many times since we went our separate ways, and we get on fine now. I guess we've all grown up and matured.

In 1978 Linwood had just acquired a new apartment in New Jersey, and it is where we live to this day. It's absolutely wonderful, on the fourth floor of a big apartment block on a hillside that slopes down to the Hudson River. It's quite rural around us; many of the houses are made of timber and have big gardens. Down by the river there are some derelict building sites, a few restaurants, but also fields of wheat and grass. Across the river lies the most glamorous island in the world, Manhattan. At night, when it's all lit up, it is spectacular.

I came out of the hospital on July 3, so the next day was Independence Day, which seemed symbolic somehow, as we stood together for the first time on Linwood's terrace and watched the Manhattan fireworks display across the Hudson River. When people ask me why we live in New Jersey instead of Manhattan, I say, "Because who wants to look out of their apartment at a view of New Jersey?"

PART THREE

I Will Survive
17

I t all started so quietly. Later on in 1978, once I was on my feet again after the operation, Linwood and I began preparations to make another single for Polydor. We had been asked to do a song called "Substitute," because the new president of Polydor, Freddy Hayan, had just had a big hit with it with a group called Clout in Britain, where he had come from, and he wanted us to do a version for the United States. In the meantime, Linwood had been listening to recordings by the music publisher Freddy Perren. He asked Polydor if we could use Freddy Perren as producer for the new single. Polydor agreed, so Linwood called Freddy Perren and the deal was made.

Freddy Perren said they would be glad to do it, providing they could have the B side for one of their own writers' songs. So that was the deal—Freddy Perren would produce Gloria Gaynor singing "Substitute," and one of their writers would write the B side. The writer, Dino Fekaris, came and talked to me, and we discussed the kind of things I liked to sing and the kind of subject matter I liked to deal with, and he wrote a new song he called "I Will Survive"—for the B side.

I'll always remember how this guy Dino Fekaris had come along to the studio, and he'd forgotten to bring the words of the song with him, so he just tore open a brown paper bag and wrote the lyrics out on that. We read it, and Linwood and I looked at each other, and I said, "We're going to put this on the B side of *what*? This has to be a hit." We knew as soon as we read the lyrics, even without hearing the marvelous music arrangement, that these were timeless words that everybody could relate to.

But the record company's attitude was not at all confident, and on its first release in 1978, "I Will Survive" was put on the B side of "Substitute." No one at Polydor wanted to buck Freddy Hayan, the new president. "Substitute" was his baby, and that's what they went with.

Linwood said, "Well, it doesn't matter. Because when you do live performances, we'll put this song at the end of the show and see what the people think about it. We'll let the public decide." Ron Kreidman, who has been our lawyer, counselor, and trusted friend for over seventeen years, was consulted. Linwood and he went to see Dickie Kline and Rick Stevens, heads of Polydor's A & R Department. They convinced them that Rick should take "I Will Survive" along to Ritchie, the very influential deejay at Studio 54. Ritchie loved it and started to play it all the time.

Meanwhile we went on tour in Mexico, and Linwood got most of the deejays over there to play the flip side, instead of "Substitute." Every time I sang, or the deejays played, "I Will Survive," the response was absolutely tremendous. Other deejays picked it up and began to play it in all the disco clubs and on the radio. I don't ever remember hearing anyone play "Substitute." "I Will Survive," the B side, was always the side they played.

Finally, early in 1979, Polydor released the song as the hit side. It immediately became a number one hit in five different countries, including the United States, Britain, and South America, and over the years it has reached number one in every country that I've ever heard of.

Next we produced the album *Love Tracks*, featuring "I Will Survive," which went gold and has been my own, and the whole disco era's biggest ever dance hit. It sold fourteen million copies in the first few months, and the following year I was awarded a coveted Grammy Award for Best Disco Record.

My memories of Grammy Award ceremonies bring back feelings of both ecstasy and agony. It's the most important, glamorous night in the music world's calendar. One year I had the honor, along with Isaac Hayes, to be asked to present the Grammy for the Best Male Group. I met up with Isaac at the rehearsal the night before, and we agreed that we didn't want to look stupid and mechanical, as you can if you read everything off the cue cards, so we took the trouble to memorize all the cards we had to read.

I couldn't decide that night whether to wear a silver sequined gown or a gold lamé cocoon dress that I had bought for the presentation. I decided on the gold lamé, a glamorous outfit with a fishtail bottom that I'd had designed for me by the L.A. designer Eileen Warren. I looked fabulous, or at least Linwood and I thought so. I was doubly pleased when I got there and saw that nearly all the other ladies were wearing sequins. I felt like the belle of the ball.

We waited backstage until it was time for Isaac and me to make our presentation. Someone said to us, "When you go out, pass the first podium and go to the second, and make the presentation from there."

Simple enough, right? Sure. Except that from where I was standing, I couldn't see the first podium. As we walked across the stage, I started to walk straight past the *second* podium, totally confident that there was another podium ahead, and thinking about how great I must be looking on camera. Isaac, gentleman that he is, gently steered me back toward the correct podium. I hadn't had stage fright since high school, but then I began to feel the first twinges of nervousness, as I realized that I had been about to make such a mistake.

We stood together at the podium, and we used the cue cards only for timing, remembering every line and who was to say what. We were doing great until Isaac said, "And the winner is . . . the Bee Gees!"

Everyone applauded loudly, and at that point a cue card came up that I had never seen before—one that apparently is always used when the winner or winners aren't at the ceremony. So I read, "Ladies and gentlemen, the Bee Gees can't be here tonight, but we congratulate . . . him, her, or them . . ." Aghh! I could not stop the words from coming out of my mouth, and it seemed to me that they hung in the air for at least half an hour, while I stood there with a death grip on the podium. I half wanted to cry, half wanted to laugh, but I felt completely humiliated. I looked over at Linwood in the audience and saw him trying to disappear under his seat. I finally said in a shaky voice that betrayed all I was feeling, "Isaac! I *told* you I didn't want to read!"

Isaac put one arm around me and with the other, prized my fingers loose from the podium. Waving at the camera, he said, "Thank you," and through clenched teeth murmured to me, "We're going to walk off to the left now." I managed what I hoped was a reasonably sane smile at the audience, and in two more seconds it was over. Phew!

Whenever I sang "I Will Survive" at that time, I was relating it to my recovery from spine surgery. The word was going around after my accident that "the Queen of Disco is dead," so one of my main thoughts was that my career would now survive. And in a funny way also, it felt as though it had to do with surviving the death of my mother. I know the song is about abusive relationships and women asserting their independence of men, and for most people that's what they identify with. I have suffered in that way myself, of course, but for some reason, I never think of that when I sing it.

It's been wonderful, because so many people have come to me with things they have survived. I've had children tell me that they thought they were not going to pass their exams; there was a man who said he now felt he wanted to go on living, on hearing the song after a failed suicide attempt . . . All kinds of people have told me different ways in which this song has been an encouragement to them. It's one of those songs, rather like "Bridge over Troubled Water," by Simon and Garfunkle, that seem to have captured the universal imagination. So I'm really, really blessed by this song. But although I have always

139

been able to sing the words with great conviction, it has still taken me a long, long time to learn the lesson of the words for myself.

$\mathcal{I}$ was in the apartment one day early in 1979, and Linwood called me from the office. "Let's get married," he said. I was in bed asleep.

"Huh?"

"I said, 'Let's get married.' "

"Okay," I said, and hung up. I lay back down. And then I woke up. I dialed him back at the office and said, "Did you just call me?"

He said, "Yeah."

"Did you just ask me to marry you?"

"Yeah."

"Did I say, 'Okay'?"

"Yeah."

So I said, "Okay," and hung up again. Which sounded cool, but belied my true feelings about the matter.

I asked him later if he had asked me to marry him because the accountants had questioned our relationship. And I asked him why had he waited so long to ask me. I wondered if he hadn't wanted to marry me earlier, when it probably seemed that I was the one who was making all the money. By this time he had his own offices on Park Avenue, he'd been offered membership in the chamber of commerce, he'd been offered membership in the National Association of Artists' Managers, he had established his own publishing company, he'd had songs released, so he had his own income, independent of what he earned from being my manager. I thought that was what he had been waiting for, so nobody would say he was only marrying me for my money.

Somehow he misconstrued my words, and thought I was asking him if he was only marrying me to keep people from saying he was only going with me for money. That's not what I meant at all, and even if I thought that, I would never have said it. But I didn't think that. I just wanted him to confirm that the reason he hadn't asked me to marry him before was that he didn't want anyone to think he was marrying me for my money, even though, as I have explained, I didn't actually have any money in the first place. So Linwood was the only one of us who had ever had any money, and now he was earning very good money.

Anyway, he got very insulted about that, and I've never been able to straighten that out with him, but I hope that he reads this and finally understands what I meant.

We set October 9, 1979, as the date to get married. It was his parents' wedding anniversary. I got in touch with Pastor Thomas, who had preached so well at my father's funeral, and he said he would be more than glad to do the ceremony.

Linwood thought it was ridiculous to have a huge wedding, and spend all that money to feed a whole lot of people who couldn't care less, and so we were going to have a private ceremony in our own apartment. The stupid thing was that, I guess because we weren't planning a wedding as such, we never thought about the things you need to have to get married. I only remembered a few days before that I didn't even have a dress to wear. I had to quickly make my own wedding gown.

Now, in the back of my mind was the thought, "He's being

very stingy." I'd always wanted a big, luxurious, and wonderful wedding in a church, with lots of friends and family there to see. But if this man was going to marry me, I was going to do it whatever way he wanted. I was terrified of throwing any monkey wrenches in the works. So we were going to be married in the living room with no one there except his mother and father, a photographer, and the minister. But the day before the wedding, I woke up to the fact that we didn't have a marriage license, we didn't have a blood test, and I had barely finished making my dress, which was nothing but a glorified caftan. It was very pretty, made of cream-colored crepe-backed satin, with champagne lace, but here I was, still making it at five o'clock in the evening, the day before we were going to be married, with no blood test, and no license. I thought, "You stupid person! How are you going to get married without all these things?" So I called the minister and told him I was sorry, but we would have to postpone it.

He said, "Look, I don't like postponements. You chose a date to get married, and that's the day you're supposed to get married, and I think you should. This is what you have to do. Tomorrow morning go to your doctor, tell him you need a blood test and that you need the results right away. He will send you to the lab and you will get your results. Go with them to the place where you get your marriage license. All you have to have is a marriage *license*. It's between you and God what day you get married. Just because the state won't confirm it until you can get its stamp doesn't make any difference—you're going to get married tomorrow." And so we did.

I Will Survive

Back in early 1979, as soon as "I Will Survive" was released in Britain, British agents seemed to be flying in on every plane to try to book me for a tour. One agent, Malcolm Feld, offered to put my show on for five nights at the London Palladium. I think what really clinched the deal as far as Linwood was concerned was that Malcolm offered, as part of the package, that we would fly over on the Concorde, a great new experience at the time. So they agreed I would go over for five days at the London Palladium in April 1979.

The Concorde was a thrill, but when we arrived, Malcolm Feld was a very worried man, because it was just over a week before the show, and he had called the box office to ask if he could reserve fifty tickets for friends, and the guy had said, "You can have as many tickets as you want." Only six hundred seats had been sold, out of a possible thirty-five thousand seats for the five nights. The guy had added, "But don't worry—we haven't had time to do the mail yet."

Malcolm didn't know what that meant, and he did worry. For about three or four days, he was phoning everyone he knew. And then, two days before the first show, he called to get 250 tickets, and the guy said, "You can't even have the fifty you first asked for." The entire show was sold out for five nights, and in the end we had to do a sixth night.

When the man had said, "We haven't done the mail yet," he had meant that because of staff illness, they hadn't yet opened the six or seven *sacks* of mail from people who had written in for tickets, and enclosed checks. By the time the show opened, there wasn't a seat to be had, and when Farrah Fawcett-Majors and Lee Majors, who were over making a film at Pinewood, wanted to see the show, the manager of the Palladium, Louis Benjamin, had to be persuaded to let them have the royal box.

Meanwhile Polydor had telephoned to say that I had gotten a gold record for "I Will Survive," and they wanted the presentation to be made onstage at the Palladium. I gave a little curtain speech when it was presented to me, thanking everybody. Then I saw Linwood at the side of the stage, and I asked him to come out onto the stage, and introduced him as my fiancé, because we had just become engaged.

He rather sheepishly and shyly walked out onto center stage, and I took his hand until he seemed more confident, and then I let go of his hand. I was still talking to the audience about him, saying how much I loved him and how he'd been so instrumental in my career, when I heard the band strike up behind me. I turned around and Linwood was doing this sexy dance called the Rock, in which you bend your knees and swing your knees and your hands from side to side. The audience gave him a standing ovation, and I was thinking, "This man's too much! He's here for two seconds, and he's stolen my show! Get him off my stage!" And he'd been so timid about coming out there! But he finally danced himself off the stage.

I've always been treated very kindly by the press, and in fact, I can only remember one bad notice, which was after one of these London Palladium shows. The reporter ended his review by saying, "Gloria Gaynor moved across the stage like a wounded buffalo." I think he must have been a rock fan. I mean, in a size 12 dress and with a sold-out show for six nights at London's most prestigious theater, how bad could I have been?

"I Will Survive" is still in great demand nearly twenty

years later, and it is the number one karaoke choice (not that that does me much good!). It has never stopped selling and being played. People just won't forget it. I rerecorded it in Italy in 1990, on an album called *Gloria Gaynor '90*, which went gold in 1991. It has been remixed and rereleased I don't know how many times in European and South American countries, but here in the United States it had never been rereleased after 1979—until now. Radikal Records has recently released an album called *I'll Be There*, which includes "I Will Survive." It was the number one song in the Australian charts again in 1996, on the soundrack of the movie *Priscilla, Queen of the Desert*, which you can also get in the States. My own favorite album, *Gloria Gaynor's Greatest Hits*, is available in the States, too, now, although it was first produced for Europe. It includes some of my favorite songs from my past albums and has a really terrific version of "Stop in the Name of Love," arranged by Kool & the Gang.

So people all over the world have taken "I Will Survive" to their hearts. As for me, I've seen the world with it.

The World Is Our Oyster

18

We began to travel the world with "I Will Survive," and Linwood wrote in my press biography that I'd changed from being a great singer to being a great healer! I always thought that was a bit comical, going a bit far, but to some small degree, I'm sure it was true. Many people *were* helped and encouraged by "I Will Survive," and I know I became a sort of role model for many young women, a great responsibility that I have always taken very seriously, and even more so since I became a Christian.

I have visited more than seventy countries, and stayed in places of awesome beauty in Australia, New Zealand, Japan, Singapore, Indonesia, the Philippines, the Middle East, South America, Mexico, some of the Eastern bloc countries, and every single country in Western Europe. . . . Of all the countries in Europe that I've visited, I think Italy likes me best. I've been to more places in Italy than the average Italian, and I've been going there every year since 1975. I've admired their beautiful Alps, their lush green valleys, their blue-green seacoast with superb beaches, the marinas, the art galleries, the churches, the architecture . . . and the food. I've had too much great pasta calamari *fritti*, too much zucchini *fritti*, too much risotto, and far, far too many rich chocolate desserts. I was a slim and lovely girl when I first visited Italy.

On one of our first visits to Italy, Linwood and I took along a friend, Norma Jenkins, from New Jersey, who was also a singer. Norma had never traveled internationally, and we thought we'd give her the experience of performing before a foreign audience. Norma is far more flamboyant than I could ever be, and whenever we entered a hotel or restaurant, I think they always thought that she was the star. I must admit that it irritated me, but I guess she did look and behave more like people expect stars to be.

One day we were in a supermarket, and we had separated. A woman came over to me and, speaking in English with a heavy Italian accent, pointed to Norma and said, "Ees that Glowria Gaynor?"

I said, "No, no, it isn't."

She said, "It's okay, you canna tella me. I no bother her. It's Glowria Gaynor, no?"

I said, "No, I assure you, it isn't."

This woman wouldn't have it. She approached Norma, and I mouthed to her over the woman's shoulder, "Don't you dare!" Norma darted around the corner of the next aisle and met me at the door, and we left laughing.

Another time on tour in Italy, the band and I were traveling on a bus through the night. I had fallen asleep lying on the long seat at the back of the bus, when something caused me to wake up. I sat up and looked out the front window, and I could see that we had stopped in front of an overpass. The driver seemed to be sizing it up. I lay down again, and then jumped up as I felt the bus race forward, then jerk to a halt. He'd charged, and jammed the bus under the overpass. The skylight shattered and glass was showering everywhere, all over the startled band members, who were violently awoken from their sleep. I warned them not to cut themselves trying to get glass out of their hair, but to wait until we got to our hotel and could use a vacuum cleaner.

It was two in the morning and there we were, with all our luggage, standing waiting on the highway for another bus, which came in about an hour and a half. We reloaded and went off again. A couple of hours later, I woke up again, and couldn't see anything out of any of the windows. The driver appeared to be hunched over the wheel as though he couldn't see where he was going, and we were creeping along very slowly. Suddenly we hit something that jolted the entire bus and nearly knocked us all out of our seats again.

It was pitch dark. There was a very, very strange noise outside the bus. As the bus doors slowly opened, we realized that it was being made by hundreds of chickens, and we were in the middle of them. The driver had mistaken an alley for a narrow street, and had driven the bus straight into someone's barn. Could all this possibly have happened in one night? We couldn't believe it.

In Britain, where I've performed countless times on both television and radio, and made many very good friends, I've had the honor of singing in Buckingham Palace, at a big charity gala organized by Ann Shelton. I've sung before the Duke of Edinburgh. We were invited to a big party at the Hilton Hotel on the eve of the wedding of Prince Charles and Princess

Diana, and I remember that particularly well, because our host gave me a £100 raffle ticket, and I won a fur coat.

*I*n 1982 we went to Egypt, a trip I looked forward to. I performed at the Mina House, from where we could see the Great Pyramid of Cheops, at 452 feet the highest pyramid of Egypt. President Sadat's daughter was in the audience that night. After the show we climbed up inside the pyramid, and marveled at how huge the stones were and the whole apparent miracle of the construction. And nearby was the Sphinx, 189 feet long and absolutely amazing.

We were taken to a party where we enjoyed a show of dancing horses. We also visited a school where children are taught to weave carpets from the age of five. These children create pictures in their minds, and weave them into the carpet as they go along, one strand of yarn at a time, across the loom. It's magical.

They said if you drink from the Nile, you will be sure to return—but it was so dirty, I only pretended. We rode horses while we were there, and one day while we were out walking we came across a man with a camel, with what looked like an offering plate in front of him. George Braxton, our drummer, asked how much it would cost to get on the camel. The man said, "Nothing."

George said, "Really? Can I get on?"

The man said, "Sure."

The camel knelt down, and George got on. When the camel stood up, the man said, "But it costs five dollars to get off!"

I Will Survive

Whenever we visit a new country, I make it my business to learn at least a few simple phrases in the native language. After all, I sing the entire concert in English, so I think it's nice if I can speak to the audience a little bit in their own language.

When I went to Lebanon in 1983, I found a language teacher who taught me ten words and phrases in Arabic—all of which I've since forgotten except *ma'haba*, which means "hello"; *shukran*, which means "thank you"; and *Ana bad aish*, which means "I will survive"; and *Ana behebak ya, Lub'non*, which means "I love you, Lebanon." I may not be spelling them right after all this time, but that's what they sounded like. The teacher said I pronounced them with hardly any accent, and we were thrilled.

We flew into Lebanon and were taken to a hotel in Biblos. On the way we passed through several roadblocks put up by the different factions that were occupying the war-torn city. I was surprised to see how beautiful and modern the clothes were that people were wearing. There was obviously still much affluence there, and many of the buildings were made of a beautiful white stone. Much of the architecture was exotic and like none I'd ever seen. There were also more familiar styles of building, big office blocks and stores like you'd see at home. The area was quite metropolitan, but marred by the holes and craters made by bombs, shells, and mortars. It was my first time in a war zone, but as we passed by, people would wave and call out, "Welcome to our country!" so it all seemed very warm and friendly.

The next day we were taken on a tour of the city. Soldiers

from the Israeli army, the Lebanese army, and the Syrian army all escorted us together. They laughed and talked with us, and with each other, so we felt quite well protected, although it was a bit worrying when one of them would suddenly shoot off his gun from his hip. Many of these armed soldiers looked like, and probably were, mere teenagers.

We were at the United Nations just the day before it was bombed. I met Andrew Young, who was then the American ambassador. We went to a U.S. marine barracks and visited the men on patrol the day before the infamous car bombing. We saw foxholes and how the soldiers live during wartime, and with every step, I thanked God that I couldn't be drafted! I had had no idea what to expect, so I was wearing very feminine white sandals that got all muddy, and a white sleeveless dress in soft fabric. I nearly froze. Would you have known it was freezing cold in the desert?

I was performing for the soldiers that night, and couldn't wait to be dancing under the hot lights. God bless the men of the armed forces who go out and have to endure so much to protect our country.

The next evening I was performing for the general public. Once again, as we drove through the city, we passed lots of roadblocks. There was an excited crowd waiting to greet me at the stadium, and the applause and cheers were deafening as I ascended a wooden stage that had been assembled in the middle of a football field. The noise only died down when the musical introductions began. As soon as they recognized each song, they cheerfully sang along with me, in broken phonetic English, and as I finished each song and ventured one of my words in Arabic, they seemed thrilled beyond measure, and called my words back to me in Arabic. "Thank you!" "Hello!" "How are you?" The response of the crowd had risen to fever pitch, and at last, at the end of the program, when I spoke the Arabic phrase *"Ana bad aish,"* meaning "I Will Survive," the cheers were deafening and they all repeated, *"Ana bad aish! Ana bad aish!"* The instruments began to play the introduction to the song, and I had saved my best until last: I was going to give them the one long phrase I'd mastered in Arabic. I shouted out to them in the best Arabic I could, *"Ana behebak ya, Lub'non!"* "I love you, Lebanon!"

A dead silence fell over the crowd. I thought, "I know I got it right. Perhaps they haven't understood me." I shouted out again, *"Ana behebak ya, Lub'non!"* Still—dead silence. By this time the instrumental introduction to "I Will Survive" had nearly ended, so I thought I'd better stick to what I knew, which was singing. So I just shouted out one more time, *"Ana bad aish!"* "I will survive!" And they all shouted back, *"Ana bad aish!"* to my great relief. I sang "I Will Survive," and bowed and left the stage with the audience clamoring for an encore. As I started to return to the stage, Linwood grabbed my arm and hissed in my ear, "Forget the linguistics—just sing!"

"Why? What did I do wrong?"

"You were saying 'I love you, Lebanon!' "

"I know. What's wrong with that?"

"We're in Syria!"

I mean, we'd been showing our passports every ten minutes to someone. How was I to know that within a couple of hours' drive from the hotel, one of those hundreds of roadblocks was actually a border that let us into Syria, where they *don't* love Lebanon? Fortunately, even though I'd told them I loved Lebanon, the Syrians still loved me.

We've been to several Eastern bloc countries. We went to Warsaw and Gdansk in Poland during the time of Solidarity demonstrations in 1982. I did a TV show in Gdansk, but although there was a large audience, they seemed tense and unresponsive. The television cameras had a hard time keeping up with me, as I reinforced their probable opinion that Americans are wild and unruly by jumping off the stage and going through the audience, encouraging them to clap and sing along. The studio audience loosened up and began to have a good time, although there were people watching who did not approve. Later that night, Linwood and I were refused entrance to our hotel discoteque. They said it was closed, but we could hear the music, and we could see people dancing. We certainly must have offended someone.

More recently, in Kazakhstan, we have learned something of the hardships endured by people living in Eastern European and Asian countries since the breakup of the Soviet Union. We saw some great contrasts. We were well received by our hosts, but they had very little. The meals did not begin to measure up to the luxury that we would take for granted even in our cheapest fast-food restaurants. Yet we knew they were giving us the most and the best that was available, and that they themselves could never afford to eat as well as they were feeding us. We tried to buy things, but no one would take the local currency; they all wanted dollars. Not that there was much to buy. The shelves in all the shops and stores were almost empty. The whole place looked as though it had been abandoned for some years, and when the people came back they hadn't bothered to repair or fix up anything. We were told that when they got rid of the oppressive government that had been taking care of them, and democracy had been restored, no one wanted to work unless they could make a lot of money. Nobody wanted to do the menial jobs of cleaning and repairing the infrastructure, so none of it was being done. The average salary was about two-hundred dollars a month.

In contrast to all this poverty, our show was held in a huge amphitheater built into a mountainside, with state-of-the-art lights, stage equipment, television cameras, and a VIP section with a television monitor for each table. The event was an international talent contest, with judges flown in from all over Europe and the United States. The contestants were all aspiring artists, and I was the professional "guest star" for the evening. All this was being paid for by the government.

After the performance we had a sumptuous meal, complete with caviar and champagne, hosted by the mayor of the city, and attended only by the international judges and promoters, and Linwood and me. Linwood and the European agent, for that show had spent all afternoon with the promoters and they had been talked into trying some Russian vodka. By the time we all met to go into the grand dinner, they were beginning to feel it. As we entered the dining hall, beautifully decorated with flowers all along the six long tables, we were formally introduced to the other judges and to the mayor of Kazakhstan, who looked like a cross between a Samarai warrior and a Sumo wrestler.

Thanks to a combination of the vodka and the high altitude, Linwood was being an even more animated version of his always outgoing self. He was introducing himself to all the people as they came into the dining room. Suddenly the mayor, sitting in the center of the top table, said in a loud voice to Linwood, "You! Sit down!"

Linwood said, "I know you're not talking to me. You don't talk to me like that."

He didn't recognize the mayor, but I didn't realize that, and I began to feel nervous. Sitting beside me was the American judge. I said to her, "Do you know what's going on here?" She said, "Well, the mayor is wielding his power, and your husband has had a little too much vodka."

The mayor stood up and said to Linwood, "You sit down now! I am dictator!"

Linwood said, "Now, you look here, boy! I'm an American. I don't have any dictator. I do the dictating."

I was tugging at his jacket and pleading with him to sit down. It was difficult, because Linwood was calling this man a "clown" and getting himself all wound up, but eventually I got him to sit down.

It eventually became clear what the mayor was doing. He wanted everyone to be seated so that he could call each country's representative one at a time, so they could introduce themselves to everyone else at once. The mayor spoke very little English, but he had an interpreter, and the introductions went on as he had ordained. When it came to our turn, he asked me to speak. I thanked him for the invitation and congratulated him on the organization of the whole event. I said I thought it was a wonderful opportunity for his country's aspiring artists to be seen. And then I sat down.

I had been the last one. The mayor stood up, and his interpreter relayed his speech to us, which ended with a special welcome and thanks to me for coming, showering me with accolades for my performance. Then he said to Linwood—in English—in the same stern tone, "You stand up!" Linwood stood up quickly, ready for anything. The mayor took his interpreter by the hand and led her around the long table to where Linwood was standing. Through his interpreter the mayor then said to Linwood, "Sir. If I have said or done anything to offend you this evening, please accept my apology. I, too, am an unreasonable man!" He then put his arms around Linwood's waist and lifted him from the floor. Then Linwood put his arms around the mayor's waist, but could only get him to his toes. The rest of us all sat and looked on in wonder as Linwood and the mayor became best buddies! Linwood became something of a local hero for the rest of our stay, and the next morning, when we went into the dining room for breakfast, he got a standing ovation.

*T*hen there was Moscow, where we stayed at the Savoy Hotel. It is as lavish and ostentatious a place as you'll find anywhere in the whole world, with glass and gilded ceilings, polished brass banisters up the great staircases, and gorgeous paintings in gilded frames lining all the walls. The dining room had live performances by artists dressed in white wigs and traditional Russian costume. The food was fantastic. I had been invited there to do a benefit concert for the sick children who had been victims of Chernobyl. We attended a party given for the children who were well enough, and of course, I sang "I Will Survive" for them. Then we went to the hospital to see and sing for the others. The next morning we spent an hour taking photographs in Red Square. At Moscow Airport we had meant to buy caviar, until we noticed, much to our surprise, it was more expensive there than at home.

I love visiting Spain and Mexico, because I can speak the language. In all Spanish-speaking countries I always sing "I Will Survive" in Spanish, and I've also recorded it in Spanish.

We have done uncountable numbers of live tours and TV shows over the past twenty years in South America. We have our second home in Mexico, and have always been warmly received by Spanish-speaking audiences everywhere, but sometimes the contrast between the life of the rich and the poor in these countries has brought me to tears.

In an early trip to Argentina I met Eddie Sierra, whom we later sponsored to come to the States and become my cowriter. Eddie is a lovely man and a terrific writer. The first thing he ever did for me was put a melody to the song I'd written as a poem ten years before I met him, called "I'm Still Yours," which eventually went on my album *Experience Gloria Gaynor*. He's written several songs for me since, some that I've yet to record.

In Bolivia I met someone whom I would have loved to have as a lifelong friend, but of whom my husband did not approve. I wanted him to come home with us. His name was Catire. He was an eighteen-month-old lion! Everyone was afraid of him, except me and his trainer. I would go into his cage and play with him. I thought Linwood would pass out when Catire took my shoulder in his mouth. I just punched him in his head and said I wasn't a meat loaf. Linwood was yelling to the trainer, "Get her out of there now, before she ends up as dinner!"

I didn't know why they were all so afraid. Catire was cuddly and lovable. But later, in the restaurant, I had to leave because they wouldn't put their cat away. They would not believe that I have a terrible, lifelong fear of cats—*little* cats.

Which reminds me of the day when I was reading the Bible and I came to I John 4:18, which says, "Perfect love casteth out fear." I prayed, "Lord, if Your love is perfected in me, please cast out this awful fear that I have of cats. I call it done, in the name of Jesus." Then I just believed that it was done. A few months later, when I'd forgotten all about it, my girlfriend's son came up behind me when I was visiting them, and just as he was saying, "Are you afraid of cats?" he dumped this huge black cat in my lap. And I felt no fear whatsoever. I had honestly and truly been delivered. Since then I've made friends with many cats; I like it when they sit on my lap, and can even imagine owning a cat, although my little dog, Diamond, whom I'll tell you about later, would definitely not approve.

In 1988, I think it was, I was in Japan, and I decided to fly home to New York via Los Angeles, where one of my four best friends, Fippy, lives. Fippy's real name is Florence Dixon. I telephoned Fippy and told her I was leaving Japan on July 3, and would like to spend the Fourth of July celebrations with her and her family in L.A. She was delighted and said she'd meet me at the airport, where my plane was due to land at midday.

I left Japan on July 3 at two o'clock in the afternoon and flew through the night 12 hours, and got back to L.A. at one o'clock the following afternoon. When I got my luggage and everything in L.A. Airport, Fippy was not there. I supposed she'd been held up by the children or something, so I waited for a half hour, and she still wasn't there. I called the house and no one answered, so I supposed she must be on the way. I waited a bit longer, but she didn't come, and I was tired of the airport, where there was nowhere to sit, so I decided to take a taxi up to her house.

There was no one there. I sat on my luggage outside to wait, when I heard a rustling noise behind me. There was Fippy's husband, Carl, digging in the garden. I said, "Carl! Where's Fippy?"

He said, "G.G., what are you doing here?"

I said, "Well, I told Fippy I was coming, and she was supposed to pick me up at the airport. Is that where she went?"

"No. Fippy went to church. Some kind of meeting they're having. But Fippy wasn't expecting you until tomorrow."

"Why? I told her I'd be in on the Fourth."

"*Tomorrow* is the Fourth."

I had left Japan on July 3 at two in the afternoon, flown through the night, and arrived in L.A. at 1:00 P.M. in the afternoon of the same day. It didn't seem possible, but if you cross the international date line backward, that's what happens!

God has blessed me to travel and see the world. When I met Andrew Young at the UN in 1978, he named me Honorary Goodwill Ambassador for the United States, which meant a great deal to me. We've made lifelong friendships, learned about strange cultures and customs, and stayed in many beautiful lands. I am still 259½ percent American, and my travels have left me with the certainty that God has blessed America. Yet travel has helped us to grow and develop a much broader outlook on life. In a strange way, traveling helps you to understand that life is very short, and that we should be living each day to the fullest extent possible.

All Sewn Up

19

I look into the mirror some mornings these days, and it scares me. I think, "Wow! I'm turning into my mother." And yet, I've always wanted to be like her. She was a good, beautiful, and talented lady.

One of her gifts was sewing. She used to make our clothes, a thing I didn't always appreciate very much at the time. I certainly never asked her to teach *me*. But just before she died, I had bought some navy blue fabric for her to make a dress for me. It was a sort of shiny material that looks like soft leather, but it isn't leather. Mamma had measured me, and cut it out, but she never got to sew it. She went into the hospital for the last time, and she died.

Afterward, as I was sorting out her things, I came across this dress by her sewing machine, all cut out, and I thought, "What have I got to lose?" So I tried to sew it myself, using her machine. It came out really well. That's how I started making my own clothes, and I've been doing it ever since.

Usually I only make clothes for wearing at home—caftans

and trousers and such. But once in awhile I'll make something for stage.

I did a show at the end of 1994 at Studio 54 in Manhattan. There's been a lot of interest in a seventies revival in recent years, so when they reopened the club, they had me there for the grand opening—I never understood why the grand opening always comes so long after the actual opening.

There was a lot of press there taking pictures, and one of the pictures of me showed up again a week later in *The Star*—on the fashion page—and the title of the article was "What They Are Wearing Now," about stars' wardrobes. I've spent a fortune in my time on top designer clothes and never made it to the fashion pages, and now, of all the things that I should get noticed for wearing, it was a dress I'd made myself.

The crowd thought this dress was marvelous. There was a designer there who has a group that she calls Plus Models—they wear size fourteen and up—and she came in and said, "Oh, this dress is *divine!*" They all made such a big deal out of this dress—probably the cheapest thing that I have in my entire wardrobe.

I copy the style from a dress that was made for me in the seventies. It has a cocoon top, with what I call a "fishtail" bottom. The top is of fuchsia sequins, and the tail is made of fuchsia satin. The first cocoon dress I ever had was one I called the Mermaid, because it was made of gold lamé with a muted gold print, with pink and blue colors mixed in.

Then I bought one by Norma Kamali, but the dress was so short in the front, I could never wear it, so I made a skirt to go underneath. I often wore it—and I'm *still wearing it*, ever since the seventies.

All Sewn Up

A cocoon is such a simple thing to make. Have you ever tried to make a paper airplane? That's how you make a cocoon. You fold it like the first fold for a paper airplane, sew up the sides, leaving enough room for your arms—and that's it. It's made. If it's in a soft fabric, it falls in feminine, luxurious folds. It's an amazing, simple, effective garment.

I tend to dress according to how I feel. I have a wide taste, and I've never been one to dress only according to current styles. If this year red and white are in, and that's what everybody's going to wear—I couldn't care less. As a matter of fact, I prefer to wear what's *not* in, because I don't want to see myself coming every time I walk down the street.

If I wake up in the morning feeling tired, I'll probably wear jeans or a jogging suit. If I get up feeling really spry, then I'll probably wear trousers and a tank top. I wear a lot of tank tops, with an overblouse. They'll be very colorful if I'm feeling really up, in bright designer colors. I *love* bright, in-your-face designer colors. I don't particularly care for muted colors. I love fuchsia and aquamarine and golden yellow, or a bright canary yellow. When I wear something like that, say a bright yellow tank top, I'll wear it with a darker overblouse, to kind of tone it down, so I don't look like a giant canary that's coming down the street.

My hair usually goes along with the way I feel, too. If I'm feeling a bit down, I often wear a small hat that I think will sort of hide me, because I don't want anybody to see me. You wouldn't look at me and think, "I wonder if that's Gloria Gaynor." But if I'm feeling bright and cheery and quite pleased with myself that day—say I've gotten on the scales that morning and discovered I've lost a pound or two—I'll wear jewelry that people will notice, and a great hairstyle. And I'll make sure that every hair is in place.

I've always done my own hair. I did, afterall, go to beauty school, and I specialized in short hairstyles and makeup. Because I loved to cut hair, I told all the young people that they would look so much more mature with short hair, and I told all the older people that they would look so much younger if they got a haircut. That way I got to cut everybody's hair.

I wear my own hair short when I'm in a hurry. I can choose, because I wear wigs. If the whole day has a lot of busy stuff crammed in, then I'll wear a short "wash and wear" wig. But if I'm not in that much of a hurry, or I'm going someplace where people have an image of me that I don't want to shatter, then I'll try to look a bit more splendid, with a glamorous wig made from long hair.

Nobody usually knows that I'm wearing a wig, unless it's in an elaborate hairstyle. The only time I don't wear a wig is when it's really hot, when I wear my own hair in a ponytail or an Afro, just naturally kinky. But other than that, I almost always have a wig on.

I remember I was once in front of Port Authority in New York. I had come from New Jersey into New York, and I think I was going up to Johnny Nash's, so it was years ago. I came out of the building and a gust of wind came along and blew my wig off. Nobody else there would have guessed it was my wig blowing up the street, because I was leaning against the building, laughing so hard. And my hair looked nice underneath, so I wasn't worried. I like my hair, except that it's very, very soft, and if I go out with just my own hair, a gust of wind would blow any hairstyle right out. And it's definitely no good for on the stage, because when I perspire it falls flat and doesn't look at all glamorous. It won't hold a style, it won't hold a curl, it's just soft and feathery. It's nice to run your fingers through, though.

I make most of my trousers because, although I'm only five foot six, my legs are the same length as my husband's—and Linwood, is six feet tall. My legs are really very long, so it's difficult for me to find trousers in the styles that I like. So I make them.

I go into the dining room, clear off the table, spread out the fabric, cut out the pattern, and make myself a pair of trousers in two hours. I make very little for the stage now, because I just don't have the time, but I still make things to wear about the house—like my caftans. I like to be loose and comfortable, but a bit elegant, when I'm chilling out at home.

Linwood likes the way I dress, but he doesn't particularly like me in jeans except when I really make everything match. He doesn't like me to dress at all sloppily, but at the same time, he doesn't particularly like me to wear a lot of makeup. He prefers me to look natural. During the week I just wear a bit of powder to keep down the shine. He hates it if I go out without lipstick. He gets that from his mother. She thinks that the moment a woman walks out the door, she ought to have on lipstick. So he likes me in lipstick, with just a little powder for the shine, and I wear eyeliner on the top and bottom, but very thin and close to the eyelid, so it brings out the eye but doesn't look like I'm wearing eye makeup. He doesn't mind my wearing false eyelashes, which I do when I'm onstage, or dressing formally for some big occasion. They are relatively short and natural-looking, so you wouldn't know I'm wearing them.

I remember soon after we first met I had done a really good job—what I *thought* was a really good job—on my makeup one night. We had gone out to dinner, and we were sitting across the table looking dreamily at each other and smiling, and he said, "You've got such beautiful eyes." I said, "Thank you."

He said, "Well, but not with all that goop on them!"

Ha! Well, thanks a lot, bud!

I think that, no matter what you are wearing, what is most impressive to people is how you feel in what you're wearing. If you feel confident, no matter what you are wearing, then you'll look good. So that's the way I dress.

Sex, Drugs, and Rock 'n' Roll

20

*I*n 1979 Linwood and I became seriously rich.

In addition to "I Will Survive" being so big, Linwood was having some success with songs by other artists in his publishing company. He never published any really huge hits, but you can still make lots of money as a publisher if the songs sell reasonably well. So he was making a lot of money, and I was making a lot of money. My contracts included a rider that two bottles of champagne were to be provided in the dressing room. Linwood loved the fast cars, crazy lifestyle, night-and-day parties that sometimes went on for weeks. He loved all the attention he was getting.

I've got to admit, I loved it too . . . some of it . . . at first. I very much enjoyed my increased celebrity as an artist and the love of the fans. As my popularity increased, I was working less and enjoying it more. We were having great fun, in with the "in crowd." We were meeting people who were bigger stars than we were. We traveled in stretch limousines with iced bottles of champagne in the back. We were invited to wild parties, and we gave wild parties, and we got into marijuana—well, we'd been into marijuana for a long time, but we got more free with it. And then we got into cocaine.

I hated cocaine. But using it was the only way I could keep up and be accepted by others. And do you know what the terrible thing about cocaine is? Cocaine doesn't care if you hate it. You must have more. It made me feel as if someone were pushing me faster than I wanted to go. Some people like that. They like "the rush." But I'm really quite a laid-back person, so it's a very irritating feeling for me, being pushed. But then, to come down from it is even worse. So you have to have more, so you can stay up—until you've been high for so long you are exhausted and have got to get some rest. For me that was usually after two or three days, and then I'd have to sleep all night and all day. Then I'd wake up and start all over again.

Everyone was doing it. Linwood is a very hyper, up person. He had the same problem of not being able to rest, of not liking the "down," but it wasn't so bad for him, because he liked the way it felt when he was "up." I'm a wallflower, rather a serious person even when I'm out with friends, but he's always been the life and soul of any party, and loves it. He also loved the attention different women were paying him. It was all great fun for him.

We suddenly had all this money, and we were not experienced enough to handle it. I began to feel myself sinking into the depths of degradation. When you have a lot of money, there are always going to be people around flattering you so they can help you spend it, people whose only idea in life is to get high and stay high. I was allowing things to happen that should never have happened.

I'll say no more than this: Linwood and I gave a lot of parties, we took drugs, we spent a lot of money . . . and we drifted apart. People became far too deeply involved in our life, and I began to feel like "one of the girls" instead of Linwood's wife. The marriage wasn't doing at all well, and I felt scared and humiliated. Professionally things were going wonderfully, but back at home I felt split in two, almost like when I was a little girl.

It was really the money and high-rolling lifestyle that came with it that brought me to the major crossroads of my life. I could either take the attitude that life was a nonstop party, with champagne and cocaine flowing from the taps—or I could start really doing something about the aching void that had been growing inside me ever since I could remember, and particularly since my mother's death.

For the first few years I kept trying to get off the merry-go-round and go to church. I'd say to Linwood, "That's it. I've had enough. I'm going to get back to being serious about God, like I was when I first came out of the hospital." I was trying to do this with my own strength, because I didn't then know anything about getting strength from God. I thought you were supposed to give God something, because God was giving you material things. I thought that God had helped my career, that He heard my list of requests every night, and expected me to do something nice for Him in return. So to repay Him, I was going to pray—even though this was still just like giving Him my grocery list every night. I was also going to be encouraging to other people, and be a good, nice person.

I very much wanted to share my gifts with people by becoming an encouraging role model for them. In the years following "I Will Survive," I released two more albums with Freddie Perren—*I Have a Right* and *Stories*—and another one independently, called *I Kinda Like Me*. All three albums included songs intended to give people a good sense of self-esteem, even though I myself had none, though I didn't know it. The songs I wrote myself were nearly all love songs for Linwood:

> *Don't read me wrong*
> *You have to know what I do, what I say*
> *I mean I'm sorry, Oh my love*
> *Some things I won't say*
> *Words get in the way*
> *Where love is the matter*
> *Don't read me wrong, I beg you*
> *Don't read me wrong, I tell you*
> *I'll make mistakes—*
> *For goodness' sakes that's just exactly*
> *What they are.*
> *Don't read me wrong—forgive me*
> *Don't read me wrong—believe me*
> *Hurt's not the plan*
> *You'll understand if you will judge me with your heart*

In 1981, on the album *I Kinda Like Me*, I wrote the title song— "I Kinda Like Me"—and a rather racy song called "Fingers in the Fire." Here are some of the words, just to let you know I hadn't gone all the way religious!

> *Dimming lights*
> *Setting up a love scene just for me*
> *Ooh, baby!*
> *I can plainly see*
> *You have done this act before*
> *Yeah!*
> *The music's low*
> *What a great producer you could be*
> *Ooh, baby!*
> *You think you're a lover*
> *I'll make you retire*
> *Now, don't put your fingers in the fire!*
> *Stop before you get 'em burned!*

I also wrote "I Love You 'Cos."

> *I love you 'cos*
> *You have so many sweet ways*
> *To bring me joy every day*
> *I love you 'cos*
> *You ignore the faults in me*
> *And how you hurt*
> *Just when I hurt*
> *Although the doctor says there ain't no reason*
> *I love you 'cos*
> *It's not just what you stand for*
> *Or what I think you are*

I Will Survive

I love you 'cos
With you my love
I feel the moon is near me
And I could touch the stars

I love the last line best:

I love you 'cos
When I am weak
You're always strong
But when you're down
You're man enough to lean on your woman

There are some songs that I thought were great then, but I'll hear them years later and think, "That really was a nothing song." But some of these songs I look at now and think, "Whatever happened with these songs?" People can't buy what they don't hear.

Between 1979 and 1982, I was on a seesaw. I would start going to church for a few months, then I couldn't stand being left out of all the good times Linwood and our friends were having. I was an outsider even at church, because I didn't then know any other Christians. So I was always on my own. I couldn't stand that, so I'd be back smoking and drinking and going to the parties and getting upset with myself and feeling guilty . . . so then, after a while, I would start going to church again. You see, it wasn't about drugs, alcohol or good times, it was about feeling left out, abandoned.

Every time that happened my husband and friends would

say, "There she goes again. Oh well . . ." Drugs and champagne. Looking back, it was as if the Devil had said, "God, huh? I'll show you how godly you are, and who your God really is!"

It got so bad that I couldn't pray at night, as I was always coming home very late. I didn't get to sleep until nearly morning or daybreak, and I was ashamed to pray. Especially since I knew that only hours later I'd probably be doing the same things again that I'd been doing the night before.

In 1982 I recorded the album *Gloria Gaynor*. It was on the Atlantic label, and was my tenth album. Linwood had written three songs for it, one called "Mackside"—about the life of luxury of the womanizing "Mack," with Cadillacs and caviar and first-class airline tickets. Also in 1982 one of Linwood's girlfriends became pregnant, and had a baby daughter. I knew this way of life was just going to have to come to an end.

The God-fearing side of me slowly began to get the upper hand that year. I was staying more and more in my room, ignoring the parties Linwood was throwing in our home. I thought that if I just went off and shut myself up in my room, everyone would feel bad about it and go somewhere else. But they didn't, not at first, because they thought I was going to come back out, as I always had in the past.

When I realized that they weren't going to stop, I said to Linwood, "Look, I've had enough. I'm not having these people here in my home half the night while I'm trying to sleep."

I tried so hard to get Linwood to stop. I thought that we were doing these things together, as a married couple, and when one of us said, "Enough," then both of us should stop.

He didn't agree with that. He began to go out more to party, which meant him staying away a lot. But at least he knew now that I was serious. They all began to shy away from me, and even Linwood found it really hard to be with me. He stayed away from home more and more. At one time he said he felt it was so bad that he thought I was into the Devil. I guess all he felt coming from me was condemnation, and he thought, "God's not like that. God is a good God, and God doesn't condemn people and make them feel bad." Anyway, he condemned me for condemning him, although I never intended to.

I can't honestly say that I wasn't a bit too zealous. I was alone with my faith, and the Holy Spirit. I had had no "discipling," no coaching on how to be a witness to anybody else. I only knew that I was experiencing a wonderful life change in God, and I wanted to share Him with everyone, most of all with my husband, who didn't want to know about it. I don't think he and my other friends and loved ones were truly rejecting the message—just the messenger.

PART FOUR

Saved!
21

*I*n 1982 I got saved.

I had gone to a little Baptist church with my godmother one day, and at the end of the service, they asked if anyone wanted to join the church, and accept Christ as their Savior. I did want to join the church, but I wasn't interested in accepting Christ as my Savior, because I didn't even know what that meant. I really only knew about God, and trying to be a good person because God had been good to me. As the people went forward after the altar call to be accepted as members of the church, they were asked to say that they believed that Christ had lived and died for their sins, and risen again, and was forever interceding at the right hand of the Father . . . and I was thinking, "What are they talking about? I don't know about any of that stuff. What is all that?"

So I didn't join the church that day. I went home, but it bothered me. I dusted off a Scholar's Bible that a girl had given me some years before. She and I had somehow gotten onto the subject of religion and had had some kind of argument about the Bible. In those days I wanted people to think I knew all about everything, but she must have realized that I didn't know much about it, because afterward she had given me this study Bible. At the time I'd felt that she had only given it to me in order to put me down in front of Linwood, because she was another one who liked Linwood, although he will deny it. So I never looked at it.

During my "religious" periods, I would read my own Bible. When I felt down, I would find a Psalm that really bolstered me, like the Twenty-third Psalm. Psalms were really the only part that I understood. I guess I must have read Genesis chapter one fifteen times. I never got further than that, because I didn't understand what I was reading. Most of the time in those days, if I read the Bible, like the time when I had been in the hospital, I didn't really understand what I was reading, but wanted to look good.

On the day I returned from the new Salem Baptist church without having joined, and felt so disappointed, I opened up this study Bible. I just let it fall open anywhere, and said, "God, I want to understand about this Jesus. I've been praying to You all my life. I believe my prayers have been answered, and I never needed any Jesus to get my prayers answered. . . ."

Looking back on that now, it sounds so self-righteous. But that's how I thought at that time.

"So I want to know, who is this Jesus person really, and how come I've got to "know" Him before I can join the church and get in good with You? If You can talk to a minister, then You can talk to me. I'm here. I'm listening. I want to hear from *You* about Jesus, because people make mistakes, people lie, people get confused, and I don't want to hear from the lady upstairs or the man down the hall—I want to hear it from You."

So the Lord began to show me . . . I looked down at the Bible and it had fallen open at a section called "Harmonies of the Gospels and Prophecies Fulfilled," which correlated the Old Testament prophecies of the coming of the Messiah with their fulfillment in Christ. God always deals with individuals one on one, and so, since I am an analytical person, what He showed me first was an analysis of the times of the prophecies, and the time of the fulfillment.

If somebody ten years before Jesus was born had said, "The Messiah is coming and he's going to be born in such and such a place, and do such and such," then I'd have said, "Mary could have done that on purpose—tried to pretend that her son was the Messiah." But when I saw that it had been prophesied seven *hundred* years before, and that many other prophecies had been made, anything up to a thousand years before, and how so many things that Mary could not possibly have made happen had come true, and been fulfilled in Jesus, then I became convinced that Jesus was the Messiah, the Christ.

The Scripture that really "saved" me was the one that says "Behold, a virgin shall conceive, and bear a son, and shall call his name Immanuel"—Isaiah 7:14. And it's repeated in Matthew, where it's explained that Immanuel means God with us. And I thought, "Ooh! God with us! If Jesus is *God with us*, then—phew! That's heavy. That's really heavy. I guess He *is* important—I mean He's *God*."

When I sat down at my dining room table that morning and the Lord used that Scripture to draw me to salvation, I didn't immediately make the connection—that when I was a little girl, these were the first words I'd ever sung on the stage, performing the *Messiah* with the high school glee club. In fact I didn't recall it until nearly four years later, in 1986, when I had some friends from the church over for Christmas, and we were getting ready to eat, and one of the girls was reading the Christmas story from the Bible, and I suddenly said, "Can I sing that?" That's when I first remembered the connection. It really makes it clear to me what the Bible means when it says, "He who has an ear to hear, let him hear." Because I'd been singing those words for years, and yet I'd never heard them.

I'd never really heard them.

I had never had any doubt about the Bible being true; it was just that I couldn't understand most of it. Now I started to really go into it. I bought books on the Bible, Bibles on tape, and books analyzing and comparing the Bible prophecies with history. The Scholar's Bible also had a section called "Foundations in the Faith," teaching how Christ is indeed "God with us," that He died for our sins, to reconcile us with God and make us worthy of having a relationship with God.

I began to sit down at my dining room table every time I had the chance, to spend an hour or two studying the Bible. I got saved sitting at my own dining room table. For two years the Holy Spirit led me through the foundations of the faith in Scripture. After a person accepts Christ as his or her Lord and Savior, and believes in her heart that God raised Christ from the dead, she is saved, according to Saint Paul's letter to the Romans, chapter 10, verse 9. At that moment the Holy Spirit comes to live and take care of that individual, to comfort, guide, empower, and teach that person to be all that God had made him or her to be. So I feel very blessed, and unshakable in my faith. I didn't get it from my aunt, my mother, my grandmother, or the lady upstairs; the Lord Himself, the Holy Spirit, began to teach me. I really believe that.

I've heard people say, "I talk to God. But I don't hear Him say anything to me!" I think there are two things that are necessary to be saved:

One is that you have got to be ready to hear and accept God's truth, and submit to it, whatever it means that you have to give up, whatever it means that you have to change. You have to be willing—not necessarily able, but *willing*—to do whatever God says you need to do. And that's where I was at that point. I was so tired of my life. I had everything that I could possibly want as far as the world calls "success." I had money, fame, and even—though it may not have seemed so to outsiders, but I knew it—the love of my husband. But there was a great void, a God-shaped void, that only God was going to be able to fill. I was ready for it to be filled and to do whatever God said that I had to do. I believe that's why I was saved, and other people who say they talk to God and He doesn't answer them are not. You've got to be willing to hear and receive the truth. Christ said, "I am the Truth," so if you receive Christ, you must receive the truth. And speaking from personal experience—that can be painful as well as joyful.

The second thing is, being saved means being born again. In order to be born again, you first have to die. Your old self has to die, and you have to let it die. Many of us want to hang on to our faults and weaknesses, because we think they make us what we are. Without them, we think, we'd be nothing. But behind all our faults and weaknesses are great gifts and strengths that you only discover when you let your faults and weaknesses go.

I believe I was born again that first day that I sat down with the Bible. I can't remember exactly what day it was, because although I knew that what I was doing was significant, it never crossed my mind that it mattered what day it was. Sometimes now I wish I did know, because it's nice to have another birthday! I do know it was in 1982.

After I had been studying the Bible on my own for two years, I felt it was time to go to church again. But this time I wanted to find a church where I could learn and grow and really belong. I thought maybe I should go back to my grandmother's old Abyssinian Baptist church, which I'd gone to as a child. I remember walking up feeling, "This is home," and as I walked in I was so excited and thinking, "Oh, glory! This is wonderful! This is it!" Nobody spoke to me—before or after the service. The next Sunday—the same thing. I thought perhaps I ought to say something to them. I stood up and I told them that I'd known this church as a child, and I wanted to join, and they said, "Oh, that's wonderful! Praise the Lord, sister!" And they gave me an application form on which to write my name and address.

The next thing I got from them in the mail was a big pile of offering envelopes. And that was all I ever heard from them. I went on two more Sundays, but still nobody said anything to me, nobody greeted me, people never sat near me, and the preacher would say a Scripture and then go on a-whooping and a-hollering. I never knew how what he was saying related to the Scripture he'd just read, and even less how it related to me. So I realized that this was not the answer. I started looking for another church.

In 1984 I went to a Christian Convention at the Nassau Coliseum in New York, given by a television evangelist named Fred Price. I had gone to the convention hoping to get Linwood saved, and had taken him with me. But instead I got baptized in the Holy Spirit myself.

As I've said, I believe that I was born again sitting alone at my dining room table at home. But now I was *publicly* baptized in the Holy Spirit, and made a public declaration that I believe in Christ and accepted Him as my Lord and Savior. The Holy Spirit came upon me—we say "comes upon," but what it means is the Holy Spirit gives you the power to do what God wants you to do, and to be what He wants you to be. After scriptural instruction, I began to speak in tongues. I had no idea what I was saying—but being me, of course, I was still there on my knees talking in tongues when everyone else had left the prayer room they had taken us to. Linwood was waiting for me outside. He said he was very pleased for me. He said he could see I was really enjoying . . . whatever it was, and he was happy for me!

A few nights later, I was praying what to do about Linwood and I thought I should anoint his side of the bed. He had been away from home again for a couple of nights. I got up and took some of the oil that had been blessed, and I anointed his side of the bed. I also went into his closet and anointed his shoes, his hats, and all his favorite clothes, and I prayed over them, and claimed the spirit of the one who wore those clothes, the one who lay on that side of the bed, for Jesus. Linwood came home later that night, but he didn't come into the room or get into bed. He slept on the couch in the living room. The next day he didn't change his clothes, he just got dressed in what he'd been wearing when he came home. He didn't change any of his clothes for three or four days. He slept on the floor, he slept on the chaise lounge or on the couch. He wouldn't go out, and wouldn't go into the closet where his clothes were. So he never got anointed.

For a long time afterward I thought it would have worked if he had only changed his clothes or lain down on the bed, but I have since learned that although prayer and anointing can create a thirst, they can't force anyone to drink who doesn't want to. God never violates the gift He gave us of free will.

What I did—or tried to do—for Linwood was spiritual. So I can fully believe that spiritual beings that we call demons kept him from getting into the bed. He probably didn't know himself why he didn't want to get into bed. He probably thought he just didn't want to be near me. When evil spirits speak to you, unless you are a spiritual person, you don't want to admit that these things exist. You accept their thoughts and suggestions as your own, and you follow through on them. Unless you read the Bible, you don't know how to deal with them. You'd rather believe that an enemy does not exist if you have no defense against it.

Meanwhile, I still hadn't found a church to belong to. One day a friend called whom I hadn't seen for nearly eight years— my only real childhood friend, Grear. Seven years earlier I had run into her and she had told me she was "saved," but at that time I had had no idea what she meant. This time when she called me, I told her that I had become a Christian and was saved, and she said, "Thank God!" She had been praying for me for seven years. So I told her that I had been baptized in the Holy Spirit, but was still looking for a church to belong to. She told me that she belonged to the Assemblies of God, a Pentecostal church, which taught that the Bible was the inspired word of God from Genesis to Revelation. That was good enough for me. She gave me the names and addresses of four Assemblies of God churches in my home state.

I went through the list, and I prayed over the list, "Oh God, help me to go to the one that I need. I've had enough of running in and out of different churches. Now, God, which one do You want me to go to? I'm going to pick one and pray that that will be the one You want me to go to."

I first thought of one that was the nearest, but then I thought, "Nah." Then I chose one that was close to my sister, but then I thought, "Nah." Then I chose another one for no particular reason, or so I thought.

On the next Sunday, I drove off to find it. It was on a street called Kennedy Boulevard, in North Bergen. But when I got there—it was an empty lot. Then I noticed from the map that Kennedy Boulevard continues through three different small cities. I searched up and down the whole length of that street, the numbers starting anew in each city. But none had a church at the address that was on this piece of paper. There was an empty lot, a derelict building, an ordinary house, but there was never a church.

Driving back, I said, "Lord, did I hear You wrong or what? I mean, I know You have a sense of humor, but with all due respect, I'm truly not amused at nine o'clock in the morning, riding up and down the longest street in the world, in the rain, trying to find this building. So tell me something." I looked again at the piece of paper, and noticed that Grear had given me telephone numbers for the churches, so I stopped and called the number, but I didn't get any answer, so I went home.

When I got home, I tried calling again and got the pastor's wife, who told me that I had gone to the right place the first time, the empty lot, but they were in the process of rebuilding the church, which had had to be demolished, and in the meantime they were carrying on their meetings at a senior citizens' building nearby.

So the following Sunday I went, and I asked God to give me a sign if this was the church that He really wanted me to be in. I got there, and nothing happened. I mean, I enjoyed the service, but I didn't get any particular sign. When the service was over a bunch of people came to me and said, "We see that you're new. We hope you enjoyed it. Did you enjoy it?" They were so happy and cheerful and welcoming; they laughed and talked with me, and offered me refreshments. I had come by taxi this time, and eventually I asked them where the telephone was, so I could call a taxi to go home. "Oh no! You don't need a taxi. Don't worry about it. Somebody will take you home." Two girls drove me home, and they asked me if I wanted to come back that evening. I thought, "Going to church twice in one day is really fanatical," so I wasn't interested, but they insisted that I would love the evening service. So I said okay.

During the evening service they had testimonies. People stood up and talked about their faith. I had never done anything like that before, but I felt I should. I stood up and said, "Um. Well. I got mugged coming into church today."

They said, "What!?"

"Yeah! I got mugged—by the Holy Spirit."

186

I told them how I had asked the Lord for a sign, and I had thought it was probably a sign that they had all been so nice and friendly after the morning service, and offered to take me home, but I had really been hoping for an undeniable sign. I had been saying this to the Lord when I came in that evening, while I was sitting down, putting my handbag on the floor. A second later I had found myself on my feet, with the spirit of laughter pouring out of me, just bubbling over . . . and nobody was paying any attention. So I had thought, "Yeah. This is the place."

They all laughed. They thought that was ever so funny, and I now knew that that was the right church for me to be in. I became a member and stayed there for the next five years. I made many good friends, including Millie Betts, who has become a lifelong friend. I joined other members of the church in many prayer meetings and Sunday dinners at her home, which she made into a place of refuge and fellowship for all the young people who attended the gospel tabernacle. I learned a lot from them all, and grew in the faith in leaps and bounds.

Now I was grounded in my faith, and nobody could shake me, and Linwood and our party-loving friends at home were beginning to realize that this was not just another episode of Gloria going off to get a dose of God, and calm her conscience long enough to come back and get into garbage again. By this time everybody knew that I was seriously committed to the Lord.

I had met the Lord, and I was getting strength from the Lord, and there was no way I was going to turn back. Every now and then I'd hang out with the crowd, but I was with them, not of them anymore, and they felt the difference. Of course,

I know that it was not enough of a difference, but they did feel the difference. I was still drinking a little wine, still smoking marijuana and cigarettes. I told myself that when I drank and smoked, I could get on a higher plane and be closer to God. But how you can lie to yourself. It's what the Bible means by "hiding iniquity in your heart." Toward the end of 1984 I went on tour in Europe. I was invited to a big dinner in London with Malcolm Feld, whose agency always booked me in England, and Gina Maher, the actress, who was his fiancée then, and today is his wife. They are both very dear friends.

On our way to the hotel where the dinner was being held, I thought, "When we get there, I'm not going to drink, because most people think that real Christians shouldn't drink." But when we got to the door of this place, they were standing there with glasses of champagne. And of course, that was my drink. I loved champagne. As I've said, I always had champagne in the dressing room to drink after the show, and used to think I was being good because I never drank it before my show, only at the end.

So when they offered me champagne at the door, I took it, out of habit. They didn't let your glass get empty. We were milling around talking while they got the tables set, and my glass was never empty. By the time I sat down, I was already a little bit tipsy. They had wine on the tables. So I called a waiter over and said, "Excuse me, but this is wine, and I've been drinking champagne. Do you think you could get me another glass of champagne?" And he said, "Of course, madam, no problem." So he came back, gave me the glass, and I sipped it and said, "This isn't champagne, it's wine."

So that was chance number one to quit, but I didn't. I

called him back. In fact, in the end, I called him back three times, and finally he came over with the bottle of champagne and said, "Is this what you were drinking?" And I said, "Yes, it is." He filled my glass and said, "Do you want me to keep filling the glass, or do you want me to leave the bottle?" I said, "Leave the bottle." Meanwhile I was speaking about Christ to a girl sitting beside me. And I was talking like this: "Jeeshush ish really the one. You know whad I'm shaying? He'sh *really* God."

The next morning, when I woke up, I thought, "There you sat, speaking about the Lord with such fervor and conviction, the only girl—the only person—sitting at the table with a whole bottle of liquor in front of you, and the only Christian— what a representation of Christ that must have been to that girl!"

I fell on my knees and said, "Lord, forgive me. I am so sorry. And if You would take away from me the taste for alcohol, for champagne, I will never have another drink as long as I live."

And that was the last time I took a drink. The Lord took away from me the taste for any kind of alcohol or marijuana or cigarettes. I had no desire for any of those things. None whatsoever. When I left the dressing room after the show that night those two full bottles of champagne were still sitting unopened on the table; I would have to take that clause out of my contract.

A New Song
22

$\mathcal{A}$nother important thing happened to me in 1984.

In church one day while we were still in the senior citizens' building, a woman stood up and started speaking in tongues. Earlier that year, at the Christian Convention at the Nassau Coliseum, where I was baptized by the Holy Spirit, I had begun speaking in tongues myself, so I was very familiar with it. It's the language that gives evidence of the indwelling Holy Spirit and allows the believer to pray totally unselfishly and directly to the heart of God. I had read in the Scholar's Bible about the interpretation of tongues, and understood it, but I didn't have the gift. I'd often heard people interpret what other people were saying, but I'd just had to stand there and listen.

This time I felt involved, but also irritated, because I could not understand what the woman was saying. Then I felt two hands on my shoulders press me firmly down to the floor.

I remember going to church with my grandmother as a child, and sometimes old ladies—they were probably only about forty years old, but they had seemed old to me—would get "happy" and start shouting and hallelujahing and swaying and falling down. It had always seemed to me that they would never actually fall down until a handsome man came around, and then they would fall into his arms. I thought it was all ridiculous.

Now here I was falling down on the floor. There was no handsome man, and I wasn't shouting "hallelujah" or anything, but there I was, on the floor. Nobody took the least bit of notice. Just before I had felt myself being pushed down, I had been protesting in my spirit about the speaking in tongues. I was saying to the Lord, "I do not know what this person is talking about. I just don't understand." So when I found myself down on the floor I thought, "This means 'shut up and listen.'" So I stayed there. I couldn't get up. I didn't even want to get up.

And then somebody started speaking in English, and I'll never, ever forget the words: "You have been seeking guidance. If you will just choose to follow me, I will take you to greater heights than you ever thought possible. I will put a new song in your heart." As soon as the person had finished speaking, I felt released. I got up, and dusting myself off, I said to my girlfriend, who was standing next to me, "Well, I wonder who that was for?" She just looked at me and laughed, and I laughed, and then we went on with the service. But I treasured the words in my heart.

A year later, in 1985, the church had moved into the new building. During a service the same woman stood up and again started speaking in tongues. Again I thought, "What are You saying, Lord? Oh, what are You saying?" But this time I was smiling, there was a gleam in my eye, and I felt so blessed.

Then a voice said, "You have been seeking guidance. If you will just choose to follow me, I will take you to greater heights than you have ever thought possible. I will put a new song in your heart."

The same words. The exact same words. I thought, "My Lord! What is happening? Why am I hearing this again?"

The next day, Monday, I went into New York for something—I can't remember what—and on my way back, I was passing by the Christian bookstore and I remembered there was a book I wanted to buy. I double-parked my car. You do not double-park your car in New York, but I ran into the store thinking, "I'll be very, very quick. I'll be in and out in no time, before they can tow me."

I was standing in line to pay for the book, and I heard the Lord say to me, "Go over to the music section."

I thought, "I don't have time."

"Go over to the music section."

"I can't do that. My car'll get towed."

"*Go* over to the music section."

So I went over to the music section. I was standing there in front of the tapes, and you could almost have said I was "sassing" the Lord, with my hands on my hips saying, "Okay, now what? I'm over here. So what? What? What? Just what?" And suddenly I saw a tape in the gospel section titled *I Will Survive*.

I thought, "Oh no! Somebody's written a gospel song called "I Will Survive" and I'm going to hate it. God wants me to sing it, but I just know I'm going to hate it."

You know how you feel, when you first become a Christian, that God's going to send you off to be a missionary in the desert or the jungle or something? And you don't want to do that at all? I thought exactly that. I thought, "God's given me this song—and I'm going to *hate* it!"

They have tape recorders there, so I listened to this song . . . and it was the story of my life. I bought the tape, bought my book, got back outside, and thanked the Lord for letting His angels stand by my car, which hadn't been towed.

When I got the song home, I learned it, and I played it for Linwood, and he thought it was absolutely beautiful. The artist was Cynthia Clawson.

After I found the song in 1985, I sang it everywhere, in my church, at live concerts, and at a big Christmas concert for BBC radio that I gave in Britain in 1988. After this concert, the BBC was impressed and Michael Wakelin, a religious program producer, flew over to New Jersey to talk to me about my presenting a popular weekly radio show on Radio 2 in the U.K. called "The Gospel Train." It's something I'm very pleased about having done. I presented "The Gospel Train" for four years, playing gospel records by traditional and contemporary gospel artists, and some of what I called "vintage" gospel, with music from as early as 1914.

It was my first opportunity to share publicly my knowledge and love of Christ with my fans in England. Until then I was known only as a disco singer, and not as a fellow Christian and church member. I did six series of "The Gospel Train" between 1989 and 1993, and two wonderful Christmas concerts at the London Hippodrome in 1991 and 1992, when I had the opportunity to work with some of the best musicians and singers in England.

Some of the music I played on the radio was quite unfamiliar to me. People in Britain don't have the same gospel music as we do here; they have their own traditions, although American gospel singers are very respected over there. Our nephew, George, Cynthia's son, who used to live and work with Linwood and me for a time, thinks gospel music, on both sides of the Atlantic, is almost always out-of-date. He says that if people sing a gospel rap number, for instance, it will sound like last year's secular rap hit, but never like the latest rap hit. Perhaps there's some truth in that—in which case we gospel singers will have to do something about it and become more independently creative. After all we are in tune with "the creator."

It was not until 1990 that I finally got to record my own gospel song, "I Will Survive," for the album *Gloria Gaynor '90* we produced in Europe, which went gold in Italy. I will definitely record it here in the United States when I make my first gospel album.

Going back to 1986, I was in bed one night, and something or someone woke me. I thought it was Linwood saying, "You have to write a song." I opened one eye and looked at the clock, and I said, "What? It's four-thirty in the morning! Are you crazy?" But when I turned over to see if he was dreaming, I realized that he wasn't there. He was away for the weekend. But I still felt this compulsion to get up and write a song.

So I got up and I thought, "Now, if I write this song down, I'm not going to remember the melody in the morning." I don't even know why I thought that, because I'd never written songs with melodies before, I only ever wrote lyrics.

But this time I thought, "I'd better get a tape recorder. It'll be quicker."

I still didn't know what I was going to sing. I sat down at the dining room table with the tape recorder, and the first words that came out of my mouth were, "You're not alone. Jesus is with you."

I completed the song and went back to bed, and tried to get back to sleep, but I felt I had to get up again. So I went back to the tape recorder and sang into it two more songs. One was called "Don't You Wonder?" which asks the question "Don't you wonder why Christians are so happy?" and the other song is called "Live for Jesus." Finally I went back to bed.

The next morning I went straight to the tape recorder and played back the songs, and I liked all the lyrics very much, but I didn't have much confidence in the melodies. I wrote the lyrics down, but I put the tape away and forgot about it.

About a year and a half later, in 1988, when I was in England for the Christmas concert, I met a young man, Frank Collins, who was doing some backing for me, who said that he had some songs that he would like to submit to me for consideration. So he came by my hotel the next day and he played some of his songs. They were all secular love songs, and one had the melody and the arrangement of American-style gospel sound, and I thought the title, "The Answer," was great. I said, "That sounds like a gospel song." He said that people often said that about his music. I said, "Well, if that's the case, I have a couple of songs that I'd like you to put a melody to and arrange for me." I gave him the lyrics of the three songs I'd written at four in the morning, and had been carrying about with me ever since.

A few months later he sent me the tape of his arrangements for my lyrics, and I listened to them, and lo and behold, they were almost exactly the same melodies as the ones I'd sung into the recorder that night. I could hardly believe it. I got the original tape out and played it, and they really were virtually the same melodies. There were only a couple of notes that were different, where I had sung a harmony to what he had written. It was really extraordinary.

The purpose of my Christmas appearance at the London Hippodrome was to launch me out of secular music and into gospel music. There were 150 media people there. I did the first half of the show singing my secular hits, and in the second part I sang gospel songs. That is where I first sang the two versions of "I Will Survive" together. I said to the audience, "I've been telling you 'I will survive,' but I've done you an injustice. I've never told you *how* to survive, how I know I will survive, and how you also will survive." Then I sang the gospel "I Will Survive." That was my last song—I went off singing, "I will survive, I will survive, I will survive."

Looking ahead is just a little bit easier
When you look at where you've been
I can believe that we can move mountains
'Cos He's carried me through
Every valley I knew
If it wasn't for Christ
I don't know where I'd be
I just know that for me
I can rest in the promise of His love:

196

A New Song

I will survive
He gave me life
I stand beside the Crucified One
I can go on
I will be strong
For my strength to live is not my own
I will survive

Sometimes it seems the pain of life
Will take over me
And I fear I'll lose again—
Then I realize that to fight to the finish
I'll just lean on the Son
'Cos He's second to none
And that the battle is already won

I will survive
He gave me life
I stand beside the Crucified One
I can go on
I will be strong
For my strength to live is not my own
I will survive

He gave me life
And with His love to guide me I know
That the past is far behind me
And His Spirit now reminds me
That through the changes in my life
I will survive

I Will Survive

Just like the lily in the winter snow
Waiting for spring
I face the darkness
But I'm not alone
I have the light
And I will grow
And I will sing
And I must sing:

I will survive
He gave me life
I stand beside the Crucified One
I can go on
I will be strong
For my strength to live is not my own
I will survive
I will survive
I will survive

Salvation Army hall, and she'd be pleased if I came along so we could meet and talk. I told her I didn't expect to be in town, but I was so I went to see her.

As soon as I walked into the place, I felt I had come home. Even before the service began, everyone was singing praises, and it seemed that everybody there was happy and loved the Lord. I found Candi, and she introduced me to the pastor, and they sat me down in the front. During the service Candi introduced me, and everybody was so pleased that I had become a Christian and that I was now going to sing for the Lord. I sang "I Give You Jesus" for them. Afterward Candi took me back to her mother-in-law's house, and we spent quite a few hours talking together.

I went back to that church in the Salvation Army hall a couple of times after that. At the beginning of each service the pastor would come out and say, "Good morning."

And everyone replied, "Good morning!"

Then he would say, "How in the world are you?"

They all called back, "Blessed in Jesus' name!"

And listening to him speak in the services, I realized that he could teach me so much about how to communicate the faith to Linwood. After two weeks I called Pastor Bernard and told him that I wanted to join his church. "Why?" he said. I told him that the pastor was really nice in the church where I was, that I loved and respected him, but I wasn't learning anymore, and in particular I wasn't getting the help I needed in how to minister to Linwood. I felt I could learn more in his church. I had already learned so much in the two weeks I'd been there, and felt I could continue to learn and grow.

He said, "Okay. Fine. I just wanted to find out if you were

flaky. Because we've got enough of our own flakes." He then asked me to write a letter to my pastor, telling him that I was leaving and why, and to give him his name. He said that the church needs every minister that God has called, and if a minister has a problem, that is causing his parishioners to leave, then he needed to know.

So I did that. I told my pastor as honestly as I could, and he understood. I joined the new church, and I've been there ever since.

In my church you have to have been coming regularly for at least a year before they consider you ready to operate any kind of ministry yourself, even something like joining the choir, which is regarded as a most important form of ministry. You are also required to take a Spiritual Growth course, to make sure that you understand what the church believes and what the Bible teaches, so that you won't disseminate anything that's contrary to the Bible.

When I first joined the church, there were some 540 members, holding meetings at the Salvation Army auditorium in Manhattan, having come from a place that the church had outgrown in Brooklyn. They had now bought an abandoned supermarket in Brooklyn and were in the process of converting it into a church, so construction was going on. Pastor Bernard believed that the Lord had told him to stay in Brooklyn, in a very poor area, where, often, is where churches are needed most. After I had been going there for a little over a year, we moved into the new building, called the New York Christian Life Center, and I was invited to join the choir. I've belonged to the choir ever since, and for me it is the greatest honor.

We moved into the new building in 1990 with more than

six hundred members, and in the six or seven years since then, we have grown to well over six thousand members. Sometimes the numbers level out for a while, such as when a large group leaves the church to form a new branch of the same ministry in another part of the city, but then we just seem to start growing again, with people traveling in from three other states to join us. We've formed two new churches out of the parent community in the last three years. It is over 50 percent male, which is a great drawing card in the community, because it shows strength. A lot of young people come—about half the congregation are in the age range from early teenagers up to thirty-five years old—although, of course, we've also got a lot of old people, and a lot of babies.

To accommodate such a large membership, we have three services, at eight o'clock, ten o'clock, and twelve o'clock every Sunday. The choir is broken up into three parts, so nobody has to be in church for all three services, and we rotate, so nobody has to get up at five in the morning every Sunday. But on the last Sunday of the month, the whole choir is there for all three services. On the other Sundays we lead the congregation in praise and worship, and on "choir Sunday" we still do that, but there are always one or two songs that the choir really ministers to the congregation.

On the second Sunday we have baby dedications, usually led by Elder Pointer, a lovely anointed assistant pastor. We don't believe in baby baptism, because the Bible says that baptism is an outward expression of having accepted Christ as your Lord and Savior, and a baby can't do that. Pastor Bernard says that if you haven't accepted Christ, you don't get baptized, you just get wet. We have adult baptism, and baby dedications in which we call the parents and godparents to take responsibility for the child's spiritual upbringing, having dedicated the child to Christ for his or her protection. You don't want children growing up thinking it's already been done. They've still got to make a decision for themselves. The second Sunday is always very moving and lovely.

On the first Sunday we generally have Communion. Once in a while something will supersede the Communion, but it's always through the moving of the Holy Spirit. The Lord has told the pastor to do something else, and he's sensitive to the time, and doesn't want the twelve-o'clock service ending at three, so we don't have Communion. The Lord doesn't say, "Do it every first Sunday or every third Sunday." He just says, "As often as you do it . . ."

When we have a Communion service, Pastor Bernard calls all of the ministry people to the front, and he and his wife, Karen, administer Communion to them, including the choir. Generally he turns around to the choir, who sit very near the pulpit, which is actually a stage, because the sanctuary doubles as a theater. He'll serve the first row of the choir, and he and his wife minister to all of the ushers, and then they minister to the rest of the church. They take trays to the end of each row and give them to the first person. Then that person passes it to the next person, and the second person serves the first. Then the second person gives it to the third person, who ministers to him or her and so on all the way down to the far end of the row. In this way we serve each other and hold on to it until we've all served.

I always read Psalm fifty-one while all that's happening.

Then Pastor Bernard says what it all means, and encourages us to ask forgiveness for anything we haven't yet asked forgiveness for while we were being served. Then we all take Communion together.

We are all so proud of our pastor. He shows the Bible's relevance to modern life. He's really brought the church to life. He says, "I'm definitely not a typical preacher. I'm not short"— (well . . . he's not tall!)—"I'm not fat, I'm not bald, and I drive a Harley-Davidson motorcycle." (His wife gave him one for his birthday.) What a man. He is such a father to us all. He's still only in his early forties, with seven biological sons, and two adopted. His wife, Karen, says that if it were up to him, he would have adopted the whole church—the entire congregation would live at his house. And yet he doesn't look the type. He looks and acts like a macho man. He's very masculine, and likes women in their place, much as Linwood does. And yet he's so very sensitive. He practices what he preaches and is a great example of the prosperity God can and will bring into every area of a life that is yielded to him.

In the summer of 1996 there was a Promise Keepers meeting in Shea Stadium, and Pastor Bernard was invited to speak there. The Promise Keepers is a Christian movement trying to show how the Christian way is stronger and truer than that followed by the Black Muslims. His speech was broadcast on AM radio, and also taped for our own church radio program, which is where I heard it. At the end of his speech you could hear one of the journalists yelling, "They're knocking down the chairs!" He had made an altar call and the people were knocking over chairs in their rush to the altar. He had been speaking on race relations. He really let them know what people of color have gone through. It makes me cry even now, just thinking about it. Afterward white people were apologizing to people of color—the Asians, the Indians, the black people—saying, "I'm sorry, I never understood what it was like for you." He really touched them. It was wonderful.

He communicates so well. When he's coming to the end of his address in a service, he'll say something like, "And so this is what's meant by that . . . and now I've got to stop." And you'll hear a groan, "Aaah!" You always hear that, because we never want him to stop. No matter how long you've been there, you never want him to stop. Every service is like a sumptuous meal.

We always bring notebooks, and it was not until I went to that church that I first realized that the church is the only institute of knowledge where most people go with no tools: no books, no pads, no pens, no paper. You can always recognize the members of our church because we bring a notepad and pen, or even a computer. People actually sit in the congregation with their laptops.

We're not an overemotional, easily excited congregation. When you read and study the Word, it brings you to a deeper knowledge of Christ. To know Christ is to love Him, and we human beings get emotional about love—but that's a far cry from everyone standing up and yelling, "Hallelujah! Praise the Lord!" without understanding what any of it is about. The hallelujah just doesn't get it. You need to have a reason for your emotion—then you can really get excited. Pastor Bernard says, "The Bible is a book of patterns and principles upon which God intends us to create a proper social structure. But these patterns and principles are like soap—they will do you no good unless you apply them." We also have an excellent church school, from first to twelfth grade.

The sanctuary holds eleven hundred people, but it's always overfull. We have a tent where they wait for the next service. People start lining up from six in the morning for the eight-o'clock service. Now there are plans to move again to an even larger site. When we have built it, the new church will be called the Christian Cultural Center, and it will have a ten-thousand-seat sanctuary, because we've been growing so fast in the last few years, there's no sense now in building a sanctuary for five thousand people. There will be a theater, a hotel, and a restaurant. There will even be an office block, so that we can disseminate Christian principles into the business world, and there will be underground parking for five thousand cars. The building we are in at present will be converted into an expanded church school.

For a few years at Christmas we put on a play, *Christ Lives After All*, which has been written, produced, and acted entirely by the congregation, members of the choir, and members of our creative arts department. The costume designers and seamstresses are all members of the congregation, as are the set designers and builders.

Pastor Bernard said that the Lord had given him a vision for the church, and it was a musical vision. He gave us what he called "a spiritual-gifts assessment," and in doing that he found that we already had in the church all the talents we could possibly need to put together a professional production.

So we put on the play. Pastor Bernard believes in doing everything for the Lord with the spirit of excellence. No secondhand scraps of old curtains or hand-me-down costumes—

everything had to be made brand-new. He also believes that God's will done God's way will never lack God's supply. So if God calls you to do this, He's going to make sure you have everything you need to do it with.

The production really is as professional as any Broadway play. We even have a playbill, in which local businesses advertise, we sell tickets, the seats are numbered, and you get seated by ushers. We have everything that they have on Broadway, plus the Holy Spirit for all.

The play is set in the future, in the millennium, after the tribulation and the rapture have happened. According to the Bible, the tribulation is a seven-year period during which God is going to allow the Devil full reign on earth. Either before this or during it, there will be the rapture, when all Christians will be taken up to be with Christ. Some Christians believe that the rapture will be before the tribulation, some think it will be in the middle, or even at the end, although I've never read anything in the Bible that made me think that Christians are going to have to go through seven years of the Antichrist's reign on earth. Our church believes in midtribulation rapture.

Lucifer, the Devil, the Antichrist, was God's brightest angel. He will appear as a very charismatic being who will come to power saying that he can make peace on earth between the nations, and everyone will believe him and hand power over to him, because they will be sick and tired of war. Once he has all the nations in his thrall, you will not be able to buy or sell anything, travel anywhere, or get a job without the mark of the beast—three sixes. I don't think it will be a stamp on the body, I think it's more likely to be an identity card that you will have to carry. A lot of people will say, "I have to have it. I have to eat. I have to feed my children," but there will be others who will call on the name of Jesus. They will be helped by finding things that Christians, taken up in the rapture, have left behind, Scriptures, prayers, and other things they have written. At the end of the seven years Christ will return to earth to save all the people who have called on the name of God.

The play is about a family living in the millennium, after the tribulation and the rapture, telling their grandchildren how it was during the tribulation. In the first year I played the part of Martyred Deedee. People try to minister to Deedee. They give her tapes, but she just doesn't want to know. But when the rapture comes and she is left behind, she starts to listen to those tapes and accepts Christ. She refuses to wear the mark of the beast under torture, and in the end she is beheaded, martyred.

I couldn't believe it when I first saw my makeup in the mirror—my face was swollen, my lips were hanging off, my head was bloody, my hair was wild as though I'd stuck my finger in an electric plug; the blood and the scars were amazing. When I came on I heard a child crying, "Oh! Mom! What have they done to that poor lady?" I sang a song called "Christ Lives After All," which is the title of the play. After the first year I was never home at the right time for rehearsals, so a fellow choir member, Marilyn Harewood, has taken the part over from me, and she is excellent. She's been doing the part ever since, and I would honestly say she does it better than I do, sings the song better than I do. I would love to be in the play again, perhaps a different part as she sings that one so well, when I know I can be home for long enough to go to all the rehearsals. The standards are as professional as any engagement I've ever been involved in, so you have to earn your place in the cast.

Pastor Bernard says that if you take home what you get in a Sunday service, and you study it, go through the Bible, look up the Scriptures, apply them to yourself, pray about them, and apply them to your life, that takes you right through to the next Sunday. I've found this to be so true, so we don't have a mid-week service.

Leaving Linwood
24

*L*inwood would say things like, "Oh, just because you decided that *you* wanted to be religious, you think that everybody in the world has got to be religious with you."

I would say, "No, Linwood, that's not what I think. I'm just talking to you about what I believe, and what I know is true."

"Yeah, yeah, you know it's true, but I know God. Don't think that God can't talk to me. You think you're the only one that knows God."

We were not speaking each other's language. I had outgrown the Assemblies of God church because it hadn't been able to help me, so God had had to pull me away from there, and now He was also going to pull me away from Linwood.

I was over in the U.K. in the spring of 1988, and while I was there I went to a Christian Convention in Brighton where the American evangelist John Wimber was preaching. A good friend of mine is the British singer Danny Owen, who was taking part, and he introduced me to Bebe Russell and her husband, Len. Bebe and I became friends immediately, and have been friends ever since. I learned how pride can trick you on the last night of that convention. We were all standing up, praying and singing. I closed my eyes and I heard the Lord saying to me, "Kneel down." I didn't. I thought Bebe and the others might think I was sort of showing off, trying to look more religious than they were. So I remained standing, with my eyes closed, singing and praying. When I opened my eyes—I was the only one there still standing. Nearly every other person in that auditorium was down on his knees. You see it was really that "Gloria Gaynor" didn't want to be seen as the only one on her knees in public.

There was less than two weeks to my next UK engagement. So, because things had deteriorated at home between Linwood and me, I decided to stay on in England with Bebe and her family in Catford. I went to their church at South Lee and was ministered to there, while I tried to get my head together.

One of the big troubles between Linwood and me at this time was that I had heard the Lord's call to ministry in music. Sometime in 1987 I had been talking on the telephone with Milly, a friend of mine, and she told me that I shouldn't sing secular music anymore. I said, "I've never sung about sex or drugs or anything like that. What's wrong with my music?"

She said, "I don't know, Gloria. I just feel like you shouldn't be doing that."

And these words came out of my mouth—I'll never forget them: "Well, as long as my music is being used to draw people into places where drugs are available and they are encouraged to drink and dance beyond moral control, then my music is being used to condone things of the enemy."

My father, Daniel Fowles.

My mother, Queenie May.

My oldest brother, Ronald, in 1965.

My youngest brother, Arthur, in 1977.

My brother, Larry.

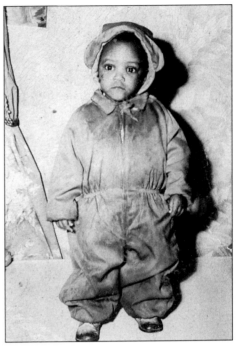

Larry and Robert (Siddiq) in 1965.

My little sister, Irma, in 1951.

The Cleave Nickerson Organ Combo in 1967.
Cleave could smell a Howard Johnson's restaurant from miles away!

City Life, featuring G.G., in 1972. I was about to sign a record contract and have my first hit.

Tera, Sondra, and Cynthia of Simon Said in 1975.
Sondra, my sister-in-law, is one of my closest friends.

David Soul in 1977, with friends.

Crowned as Disco Queen in 1979.

With Merv Griffin.

With Malcolm Feld in 1979.

Lebanon in 1983. This was my first time in a war zone.

With Regine and Michael Caine in 1982.

With Engelbert Humperdinck in 1986.

With Linwood, meeting the Pope in December, 1995.

*With Cliff Richard following the BBC
Christmas Concert in 1993.*

With Oprah in April, 1996.

With Magic Johnson and Lionel Richie at a fund-raising seventies' costume party.

And with Denzel Washington.

My favorite publicity shot!

As I heard my own words, I said, "I'll call you back." I hung up, and I immediately got on my knees in prayer and said, "Lord, is that how You feel about my music?"

The Lord said, "Yes."

"So I can't do it anymore? I'll clean up my lyrics, and I'll put a gospel song on every album."

The Lord said, "No."

"Okay . . . then . . . I'll make sure that the record company allows me to put *half* gospel, and half secular."

And the Lord said, "No."

"Okay. Well, then I'll just have to stop singing altogether, except gospel music."

And the Lord said, "No."

So I said, "Well, what do You want me to do? I don't know what You want me to do. Well, I'm not going to do *anything* until You let me know what You want me to do."

And the Lord said, "Right."

So for a year I hardly sang at all, except in church. Linwood thought, "She has truly gone all the way crazy. I have stopped being a policeman short of my pension so I could work for her career. I've taken all of my life savings and spent them on her in the hospital. I have married her and brought her to live in my home. I have wrapped myself up in her, her life has become my life. And now she's just going to pull the rug out from under me. She just doesn't care about me, or anybody else. All she cares about is this stupid church and what this preacher's telling her. And now those stupid people are telling her that she can't sing her music, that she's got to stop now . . . and she's just going to kill me." He saw it all as happening to him, that I was being given bad advice that was quite unnecessary and that was grossly damaging to our relationship and our lives.

Linwood is an emotional man. I was really stepping on his manhood and pride. I was saying, in action if not in words, that I really didn't need him anymore. I didn't realize, and God knows I'm so sorry, because I did not understand what I was doing to him as a man.

Linwood, although not a born-again Christian, does understand that I am the image of his glory. He does understand that a woman is representative of the man that she's with, because the man is to guide, guard, and govern his woman, nurture her, and help her understand the ways of the world, and grow her up in the things of the Lord. And if he can't do that, then he feels inadequate as a man. I was feeling like a victim because of some of the things he was doing, but he was also feeling like a victim.

He was right in one thing—all I was interested in *was* what God wanted me to do. He didn't see it as that—he saw it as what the *church* wanted me to do. I honestly didn't know for sure at that time what the Lord did want me to do. The only thing I was sure about at that point was that, as far as my music was concerned, He would have me do nothing. I was to learn about Him. Get rooted and grounded in my faith. Learn what He wanted me to do about my music. So that when I was released to go back to it I would be certain of my purpose and His will.

Linwood was saying, "I understand that you want to sing gospel music. That's fine. We'll spend a few dollars, make a gospel album, you'll be happy, God will be happy, and then you can go on making money with the *real* music." But I knew that wasn't the way it was supposed to go.

My mother said to my brother one day, "You know, Ralph, it's getting warmer outside, so why don't you take the lining out of your raincoat, and have it cleaned?"

So he went to the cleaners. Weeks later it was raining, and my mother said, "Why don't you wear your raincoat?"

He said, "It's dirty."

She said, "No. It can't be. I told you to get it cleaned a long time ago." He'd only had the lining cleaned!

With the Lord, you need to take time to understand what he's saying. You have to develop a one-to-one personal relationship with Him, in which you get to know His voice, and the way He deals with *you* as an individual. You may hear something and run off and do it, but if you haven't really understood what God was talking about, you can do things that really hurt people, and make people feel scarred and betrayed.

I had stopped singing secular music, but I still believed God was calling me to a ministry in music, and I started looking around for a record company that would record me singing gospel music. I found out about a record company in England. I contacted them while I was over in England in the spring of 1988, and we arranged for me to do a big Christmas gospel concert, a "Farewell Secular Music, Hello Gospel" concert, to be recorded and broadcast by the BBC.

I did not at first realize that the director of the music company intended to both book me and manage me, and try to sidestep both Linwood and Malcolm Feld. I wouldn't have let that happen, but I did think that he should be involved because neither Linwood nor Malcolm knew anything about gospel music. They needed help. I was to discover to my detriment that this guy could have learned a great deal from Linwood.

He told me he had all sorts of well-known gospel artists on his books, when all he actually had was a string of unknowns. He was probably desperate to get me on his books, and he even told the BBC that he was my agent, sidelining Malcolm Feld. He got all the money for the BBC contract, and caused me no end of trouble. So my first experience of Christian music management was fairly awful.

As I've mentioned, I did do the concert that Christmas, although there were terrible fights over money. I really missed Linwood, whom I had hardly seen all that year. And I had a cold. The first part of the concert was all secular music, and the second part was all gospel music. During the first part I almost completely lost my voice, but as soon as I came back for the second half and began singing the first gospel song, almost miraculously my voice came back.

Partly because of my unhappiness about Linwood, I was in England for a good part of 1988. Three weeks before the Hello Gospel concert, I had completed another series of engagements over there. I wanted to stay and spend more time with my friends at Bebe's church, because they had been really helping me, but I thought that Linwood would probably want me to come home. I talked to Bebe about it. (Bebe, by the way, is called that because the actress Bebe Daniels was her godmother.) She called me back later and said, "Well, we've discussed it and we've prayed about it, and we feel that the Lord is saying that you ought to stay here, and stay in the home of Martin and Jenny Hemmings."

I didn't know Martin and Jenny Hemmings. Bebe said that she was finding it difficult to tell me that I should stay with them, because she knew that Martin and Jenny had moved into a new house and that it was an absolute wreck. Martin was in construction. They had ripped up the floors, torn all the wallpaper down, and knocked down a wall of the kitchen to expand the living room. The house was a mess. But they had all felt that that was where the Lord wanted me to stay. So I said, "Well, if that's where the Lord wants me to stay, perhaps He's not finished humbling me. I don't feel any check in my spirit about it, so I guess that's where I ought to stay." So I called Linwood and he said it was fine by him. Then I went to meet Martin and Jenny.

When they had bought the house they had told the Lord that it would be His house, and that they would always take in anyone He sent to them who needed refuge. But they were petrified when they heard that they were meeting "the great Gloria Gaynor," a "star," and wondered whyever I would want to stay with them.

They took me up this horrid staircase. Their own room was terrible, dust everywhere. But my room was lovely. Because it was to be a house of refuge, they had decided that the first room they would get ready would be the guest room. It was freshly painted and all done up with Laura Ashley fabrics, with a matching border around the ceiling, a really pretty room.

Jenny was a teacher and Martin was in construction, so they were away all day. I could spend the whole day with the Lord. I would get up in the morning and shower and get dressed. I would pull a chair over to the window, sit there looking out at the blue sky, and talk to the Lord. I would read the Bible and Christian literature. I would go downstairs and play Christian music on the stereo, and stand and sing praises to the Lord.

After two weeks I called Linwood and said I was coming home. He said, "You've been there for two weeks! You had three weeks to come home, and now all of a sudden, after two weeks, with only one week left, now you want to come home?"

I said, "Yeah, I want to come home."

"Why?"

"Because I want to come home. I miss my home."

"Well, who's going to pay for you to come all the way over here and go all the way back? Who's going to pay the fare?"

I said, "I have my ticket to come home. The people who have booked my next engagment are going to pay my way back and home again."

"You don't know that."

"They are. They are. They don't even know that I've not gone back home. They expect me to be at home, to come from home. So they're going to pay my way over here and back."

"They're not going to pay *nothing*. You don't know what you're talking about, and I don't think you should come home now anyway."

So I just hung up. I got to thinking, "Has he got somebody in my house? Somebody he doesn't want me to see?" I started to become convinced that he had someone there, was having

218

an affair. I didn't know what was going on, but he seemed to be so adamant that I should not come home. I really didn't want to run into anything that I didn't want to see.

I went up to my room and closed the door, and as I did so I heard the Lord saying, "Go home. *Now*."

I made my reservation that night. I didn't call Linwood again.

When I got home the doorman came out to the cab and loaded up all my stuff on the cart. I went on up in the elevator and rang the doorbell to our apartment, because I had left my keys behind.

There was no answer.

When I had arrived I had looked up and seen that the terrace doors were open and the lights were on, so I knew Linwood was there. I started knocking. No answer. I rang, and I knocked, and I rang, and I knocked. Then I went back downstairs and told the doorman to call the apartment and tell my husband that I was at the door. The doorman said, "Oh, he just came in, so I told him that you were home."

I thought he must have driven past the door and gone into the garage to park, and that he'd be arriving any minute. I went back up to meet him at the door. I'd left my luggage on the cart outside the door. But still Linwood didn't come. I thought, "Did he pass by my luggage and go into the house and close the door?" I rang the doorbell and I didn't get any answer. Knocked, and no answer. Then I heard the telephone ring— once—so I thought he must have answered it. I thought, "Ah! That's how to get his attention!" I went down to the next level where there's a public telephone, and I called. The phone rang and rang and rang. No answer. I thought, "I guess when the doorman told him I was here, he left. He didn't want to see me."

Next I called my niece, my eldest brother Ronald's daughter, Veronica, and asked her to come and get me. It took her a good forty-five minutes to get there, and still no Linwood. I put my things in her car and went to her house. I spent the night there. I called Linwood all evening long. No answer. And all the next day and the next day, and no answer. The third day, finally, I got him.

I don't remember the conversation at all now, but I do remember that Linwood did not give me the feeling that he wanted me to come home. He certainly didn't say he'd come and get me. I thought, "He doesn't want me to come home, and I'm not going home just to get locked out again." So I stayed on with Veronica.

A week later I had to go back to England for the Christmas concert—and after all I'd been through, it was not surprising that I had a cold. Then I flew back to New Jersey, and went back to Veronica's. I didn't even try to go home.

I called Linwood a few days later and asked him if I could come and get some things. He said, "Yes, but I'm going out now."

This went on for six weeks. I kept on calling and he kept on making excuses to stop me from coming around, and finally I said, "Well, why don't you leave the keys with the doorman, and I'll let myself in."

He said, "I don't trust you."

"Trust me? Not trust me to do what? Come into my own house?"

"I don't trust you. You have to come when I'm here."

"Okay, fine." But I kept calling him and not getting any answer. Finally I lost patience. I said, "Look, I've got to have my clothes. I've only got the clothes that I took to England with me. I can't go on like this."

I got a locksmith to come with me and take the lock off the door. And I also went with moving and storage people, and took along a friend who was a policeman. I wanted a legal witness in case Linwood accused me of taking something, or we got into a fight or whatever. I just couldn't understand why he wouldn't at least let me get my things. The locksmith drilled through the metal door, making an almighty racket, and finally got the lock off.

We filed in. The house looked like a dungeon. You could feel the gloom. Linwood had removed anything that would indicate that I had been there, all my trophies, awards, photos, gold albums. . . . He hadn't put anything in their place, and the house was dark and gloomy. I thought, "He's all but buried himself in this apartment."

I told the removal people what was mine, and started moving things out. I only took things that I knew Linwood wouldn't use—the Mixmaster from the kitchen and things like that.

And—he was there! He was asleep, with the bedroom door closed. When you are in the bedroom with the door closed, you can't hear. Well, I do hear, but he never hears anything. It was obvious that on the five or six occasions that I'd come around before, when I'd seen his car but he hadn't answered the door, he'd been there. Asleep in the bedroom.

I woke him up and said, "Linwood?"

He woke up with a start and yelled, "How did you get in?"

"Well, you know, I've called several times, and I've been trying to get into the apartment, and you never would let me in. You wouldn't leave the keys downstairs for me . . . and I need my things."

He kind of heard that, and didn't hear it. Linwood doesn't wake up very coherent at the best of times.

I went into my closet and gathered my clothes together. When I was carrying them through, we met in the hallway between the bedroom and the living room. We looked into each other's eyes and I suppose he saw the love in my eyes, and I certainly saw the love in his. But I also saw the confusion. I said, "I don't understand, either, Linwood." And I just passed by him, picked up the rest of my things, and left.

On My Own

25

I wasn't nearly as anxious or upset about the separation as you might have expected. I just knew that the Lord was going to show me what was supposed to happen. I never thought I wasn't ever going back to Linwood, never saw myself as living the rest of my life without him. I thought that even if things got so bad that we got divorced, we would somehow get back together again one day. It happens all the time. But I felt that if and when we got back together, there would have to be a lot of changes, and there would need to be some ground rules set. I had come to the conclusion that the Lord had made this separation happen and it was for both of us to grow in a way that we would never have done together, to end the codependency that existed between us.

The Lord showed me a sort of a vision inside my head. There was a baby in a crib—my baby—and a doctor was leaning over the crib trying to give him an injection, because the baby was ill, but I was trying to stop the doctor because the injection would hurt, even though it would make the baby well.

It seemed to me that with this vision the Lord was saying to me, "You're trying to protect Linwood, as if you think I can't."

I stayed with Veronica for several months in her two-bedroom apartment. She slept in one bedroom, her kids in the other, so I was sleeping in the room with my niece. It was very awkward. I mean it was a nice apartment, but my niece was a young girl, she had boyfriends, and I was well and truly cramping her style. But she allowed me to stay there for several months, knowing that I had nowhere else to go.

I came to see that the Lord had engineered my separation from Linwood, because during that whole year, in spite of all the discomforts and some really uncomfortable financial problems, I was drawn into a wonderful communion with God. I needed to learn to trust God, in order to be able to do what He wanted me to, and not to be so swayed by what other people told me He wanted for me. He's not going to tell somebody else what He wants for me without first telling me, so any word that comes should only be confirmation of what God has already told me.

Veronica would set the alarm for six o'clock in the morning, although she never got up until seven. The clock would then go off every ten minutes. It got so irritating that I decided to get up as soon as it rang at six, and put on my sports clothes and go out and jog or walk. I did that every morning, walking for miles. I would walk and pray during that hour. When I got back I would read and study the Bible and study other Christian literature.

Then I started to get up even earlier, at five o'clock, and go into the living room with pen and paper. In the dark I would write down the things I thought the Lord was saying to me, sort of subjects to talk about later. I started a journal. I prayed for an hour, then I'd walk and pray for another hour, then I'd study for an hour. During the day I'd straighten up the house, do the laundry, get in groceries, and start dinner for Veronica and the kids. In the evening I would take another hour to stand in the room and sing praises to the Lord. That was how I spent my days—praying, studying, housework, praise, and worship. That was my entire day. After dinner when the family was watching TV, if it wasn't something I was interested in, I'd go off alone again and go over my notes. It was really wonderful and it helped me to grow as a human being. It helped me to clear my mind about what was good and what was bad—because some things we call bad, the Lord doesn't call bad at all. The Lord only calls sin those things that are destructive to ourselves or to His creation.

But after a while, Veronica quite understandably got restless and began to let me know in no uncertain terms that I had outstayed my welcome. I realized I would have to be moving on, so I called Candi Staton and her husband, and asked if they would ask his mother, Mrs. Marion Brown, if I could stay with her for a while. She lived alone in a three bedroom house with a livable basement. She'd said how lonely she was when I had first met her there. But at the same time she'd been talking about how she didn't want anybody else living in her house. I thought that if her son asked her, and she felt *more* that she didn't want anybody in her house than she felt lonely, then it would be easier for her to say no to him.

He called me and said, "My mother says that she will not allow you to steal her blessing." In other words, yes, I could stay with her, but I couldn't pay. As it turned out, she was ill

225

and really needed someone to be with her. She would have these spells when she'd feel as if the room were spinning, and once or twice she'd had a turn in the car while she was driving, and become totally disoriented. I drove her back and forth to the doctor for nearly three months, until she began to feel better. Then she went back to work and was able to drive again on her own.

In the basement of the house was a room where I could sing and study without disturbing anyone. I would go downstairs and sing for hours at a time, and listen to tapes of teachings. Candi and others ministered to me by sending me compilation music tapes so I could learn to sing a wide range of gospel music.

At my first church Pastor Sobey had once told me about a girl who had become quite cross because she was never chosen to sing to the Lord in the choir. He had said to her, "The church is open every day." That spoke to me. If I wanted to minister to the Lord, I didn't need a human audience. The Lord would hear me. The Lord says He inhabits the praises of his saints, and I really felt His presence so strongly when I did that.

There's a crystal chandelier in our living room, and once when I was singing praises to the Lord, for a few seconds it suddenly looked a hundred times brighter; all the colors sparkled and shimmered and I felt as though the Lord were inhabiting it. It was really wonderful.

After I had been staying with Marion Brown for about three months, Veronica had to go into the hospital for an operation. Luckily it was by now the summer of 1989, and her children were away staying with their father for the holidays, so she didn't have them to worry about, but she didn't have anybody to look after her when she came out. So she called me collect, from the hospital. Unfortunately I was out, and Marion Brown wouldn't accept the charge. I came home and she said to me, "Your niece just called you collect. But I don't accept any collect calls on my bill."

I said, "But I told you she was in the hospital. I've no way of getting in touch with her to find out what she needs, whether she needs me to go there, whether she needs me to collect her. I've paid all my telephone bills here. She calls collect, and you won't accept the charge?"

"I don't accept collect calls on my bill."

"And you call yourself a Christian!"

I was livid. She had started to get not so nice in other little ways. I had driven her around for hours, to see her doctor and such, but she hadn't let me borrow the car one day when I needed to go somewhere. I had asked her, and she'd said no, so I never asked her again. I always took the train. I didn't want to be judgmental, but I felt that this was the last straw.

I took the train and the bus into New Jersey to see Veronica, and she was ready to leave the hospital. She didn't like what they were planning to do to her, and she was ready to get out of there, but she needed someone to take care of her.

The next morning Marion Brown said, "I'm not used to people talking to me that way in my own home. So I think it might be time for you to find yourself somewhere else to stay."

I promised her I'd leave that night. I went back to Veronica's, but I didn't know how long I would be able to stay there, or what would happen next.

I Will Survive

Before I end this chapter, I want to give you Linwood's side of the story, so you'll see where he was coming from. He never understood that I felt that he had locked me out, because he hadn't actually locked me out.

When the doorman had said to me, "I saw Mr. Simon and told him that you'd just come in," well, he had seen him and told him that, but Linwood had thought he'd meant I had just come in *at the airport*. He had immediately driven off to the airport to meet me. And that was why Veronica was able to come and get me and take me away and he still hadn't come back. When he arrived at the airport and didn't see me, he went around trying to find out about my flight—what time it had landed and all of that. He'd parked and gotten a cart, expecting to help with my luggage. I wasn't there. By the time he'd got back, my niece had come and taken me away. He didn't know that I didn't have my own key, so he thought that I was playing games to get him away from the house while I went in and got what I wanted and left. He didn't know that I wanted to come back. He thought I was "just being a silly woman. She'll be back." He was thinking that if I was going to walk out on him like that, he wasn't going to beg me to come back, while I was thinking that if he had locked me out of the house, I wasn't going to beg him to let me come back. If I'd just said to him, "I want to come home," then he would have been there.

But I didn't know all this. I thought, "This man has lost it!" Some friends did say to me, "You know, this man is just sitting waiting for you to come back. He's not doing anything." A friend of his who lives in our building said that he'd go and see him and say, "Come on, man, let's go out," and he would tell him, "No, man. I miss my woman, man. I miss my woman."

Linwood just wouldn't do anything, wouldn't go anywhere, not for Thanksgiving, not for Christmas.

I don't believe that either of us doubted our love for each other during that whole year of separation. I believe that the Lord engineered it, so that we would grow. There was no other way we were going to separate. We were going to just take each other's garbage. I really loved him. He really loved me. He thought I was disrespecting him, and I thought that he was disrespecting me, but we still loved each other. Neither one of us had the nerve to say, "Get out!" or "I'm leaving!" so we were never going to grow. I absolutely know that the Lord told me to "Go home NOW."

He knew what was going to happen. I would be alone and have time to stop and think. He wanted me to stop trying to blunder my way into a gospel-music ministry, doing everything my own way and running ahead of Him. If you run ahead of God, you end up there alone.

I'm Still Yours

26

I never thought you'd haunt me
The way you seem to be
I thought that when you let me go
That I would just be free

In September 1989, while I was staying with Veronica for the second time, a girlfriend, Carol Williams, called to say she was getting married. We'd both known her a long time and were very fond of her. She said, "I want to invite Linwood. Do you mind if I send him one invitation for the two of you? I'd really love you both to come."

I said, "I guess I don't mind, if he doesn't."

Linwood and I had been talking once in a while on the telephone by now. We were quite friendly, but we still never discussed getting back together. Carol sent him the invitation, and he called me and asked if it was okay if we both went, and of course, I said yes.

Just before the wedding, I saw a very good-looking man walking down the street one day, and thought, "Gosh!" but

Linwood said in his gruff, macho voice, "Nah. I don't have a problem with that. I'm just a sentimental man. That's it."

This was now the end of October, and I was about to go back to the U.K. for my first gospel tour, which Malcolm Feld had helped me set up, and now Linwood was coming with me. It was the first time we'd been together for over a year, and of course, we would be traveling as man and wife. The counseling sessions were good. After the second meeting, the pastor said, "Call me when you both feel ready to come back." I wish now that I'd said, "No, let's set up the next meeting right now."

Linwood and I were communicating, we had had a reconciliation, but I didn't realize then that we still didn't have a full restoration of trust in each other. I didn't understand the difference between reconciliation and restoration, or that you needed both before living together again. I did actually say to him, "I think we should finish the counseling sessions with Pastor Bernard before we get back together, because I'm afraid that if we don't, it's going to end up the same way. I want us to set up some ground rules, and commit ourselves to them." And he said, "Okay." I wish so much now that we'd stuck to that, or that I'd taken up Pastor Bernard's offer of the church helping me with a loan to set myself up in separate accommodations until Linwood and I had really worked this thing through.

But we didn't. The gospel tour took us off. We spent November and December in England. We spent Christmas with Bebe and her family in Catford, and when we came back in January, I went back to my niece's, collected my things, and went home.

We started off wonderfully. Linwood was cooking, help-

233

ing me in the house, vacuuming the floors, taking out the laundry, taking out the trash, and shopping, and doing all the things I'd always wished he'd done. We were communicating much better than before. I didn't feel he was going to run out the door every time I said anything about the church. Linwood became much more considerate and thoughtful than he had ever been before. I hope he found me easier to live with too.

We didn't get out of our grievances straight away. I was still full of resentment, still unable to trust Linwood because of the things that had happened. I did believe that he was through with drugs, and he'd nearly stopped drinking. He'd stopped partying all night . . . but he would still spend some nights out, and then come home as if he'd just gone out to the post office. After he'd done it a few times, I went to Pastor Bernard and told him, and he said, "Well, you know he's testing you. Trust has been broken, and now you'll have to make a decision, and do something about it." So I told him it was unacceptable behavior and I wasn't going to have it. He continued to do it anyway. Things began rapidly going downhill again. He felt that I wasn't trusting him, that I was disrespecting him, and I suspect he was also a little bit jealous of my relationship with Pastor Bernard, which he didn't understand was like a father to daughter.

I was also back to tithing, so here I was giving this preacher all our money, as far as he was concerned. He had gotten me straight back to work. In the year that I'd been on my own, I'd hardly managed to get any engagements for myself, but as soon as we were back together, I was back working, because he's an excellent manager. Pastor Bernard explained to me, "When you left him, you took away his credibility with the people who worked with you. Okay, your marriage broke up, but they'd still want to know: Why is he not managing you anymore? You took away his credibility." That was restored when we got back together and started working again. Money was coming in, things were better financially, but he didn't like my tithing at all. We really couldn't get it together. Because the days were strained, the nights weren't absolutely fantastic either. I blamed Linwood, but I had to learn that I still had a lot of changing to do myself.

Under New Management
27

One day in 1990, a complete stranger had ministered to me. Not even knowing what I did, that I was a singer, he had just walked up to me out of the blue and had said to me, "No, he will not manage you. No man will share my glory."

I didn't understand at first, but then I thought he was talking about Linwood, particularly as we were still having such problems. I told Pastor Bernard, and he said, "Well, is he honest?"

"Yeah."

"Is he capable?"

"Yeah."

"Is he conscientious?"

"Yeah."

"So whyever would the Lord say that he wasn't to manage you?"

But several well-meaning Christian friends kept saying to me, "Blessed is the man that walketh not in the council of the ungodly," using that Scripture to back up their belief that Linwood, who they thought was ungodly, ought not to be managing me. I was thinking, "But how could I do that? How could I not let him manage me? He's going to think I'm pulling the rug from under him again, that I don't really care about him. Can God really be asking me to do that?" I also thought in practical terms, we had a management contract, and I didn't have the money for a lawyer to help me break it. It all seemed far too difficult.

Yet so many things were coming together that seemed to confirm what people were saying. Scriptures kept coming at me. I was talking about it with somebody one day, and I said, "But he's done so much for me. How can I do this to him? How can God ask me to do this to him?"

They answered, "Perhaps the Lord is saying, 'And what have I done for you?' "

I thought, "My God, I don't know what to do." Then I thought, "Before I accepted Christ as my Savior, I was putting Linwood before God. I was doing things that I knew I had no business doing. I was doing things that I knew—even before I knew Christ—God did not want me to do. But in order to hang on to Linwood, I went against God. I can't do that anymore."

I had already faced that with the tithing, by insisting that I was going to tithe, whether he liked it or not. So that way I had made my decision not to put Linwood before God. And now I thought God was testing me again, and I was not going to fail. I wrote Linwood a letter telling him why he could no longer be my manager, that I was going to take our contract to a lawyer and I was going to have it broken. This was 1990, the day before New Year's Eve, and I asked the Lord for a sign as to whether I should wait until after New Year's to give him this letter. The night before New Year's Eve I folded up a wet cloth and left it in the bathroom, and I said to the Lord, "If this cloth is completely dry in the morning, then I'll know that You want me to tell him right away." I woke up in the morning, and the cloth was bone-dry. But then I thought, "Oh, it's just dried up overnight." So I left the same cloth, which was dry, and said, "If it's wet in the morning, then I'll know." I woke up the next day—it was sopping wet.

So on New Year's Day I gave him the letter, and he read it. He looked at me in total disgust and just threw the letter aside as if he was just going to ignore it.

I remembered another friend of mine, who had been under contract with her husband, and when they broke up, she hadn't been able to break her contract, but she went on working anyway, without him, and she never heard from him again. So I thought that was the way God was going to work it for me.

One day Linwood said to me, "I'm going to find somebody to buy out your contract. You want another manager? Fine. I'll find somebody to buy out your contract. And I hope you do well."

Every now and then, every six months or so, I'd ask him, "Did you find somebody?" Months went by. I didn't know what to do. I was still working with Linwood and doing engagements. I was also still hearing from people that the only reason I wasn't taking any action was that I was scared, and that God would help me if I would just go ahead and do it. I kept saying, "But nobody's telling me *how* to do it."

"Pray to God for a good lawyer, and the lawyer will tell you what to do to get out of this contract" . . . "God wants you to get out of this contract because you cannot keep working with him" . . . "You're concerned about your marriage and putting your marriage before God" . . .

Aaagh! They kept on telling me all this stuff, but I still didn't know what to do. I thought, the Bible says wives submit to your husbands.

Pastor Bernard's words began to ring in my ears: "Why would God tell you that he can't manage you?" It was not as if Linwood were telling me to do anything that was not of the Lord. Had I *tried* to do more gospel music, to see what he would say about it? Linwood had actually been saying, "Sure, you can do a gospel album. I'll find you somebody to help you do a gospel album."

In spite of this, I hardened my heart. I must have been feeling more bitter than I realized. I felt that I had given him fair warning. I finally went to a lawyer who said to me, "This contract is ironclad. He has everything for himself, and he has promised you nothing. All it says in this contract is that he will do his best. Whatever that might mean."

I said, "Well, I really honestly feel that he has been doing his best. I've always felt like that was guarantee enough, because the more he did for me, the more would be done for him." Also, Linwood had always shown integrity in business.

"Well, whatever you thought, this contract is ironclad and there's no way out of it."

In 1992 Linwood asked me for a divorce. I went into the kitchen and sat down and said, "You've got it."

He said, "Contrary to what you think, we *will* be working together. Now, this divorce can be nice and easy, or it can be nasty. It's up to you."

239

I said, "No problem." I went into the office and called Pastor Bernard and told him that Linwood had asked for a divorce.

He said, "Really? How do you feel about it?"

I thought for a second and then I said, "Free at last! Free at last! Thank God Almighty, I'm free at last!" Then I laughed. I said, "You know, Pastor Bernard, I don't know how I'll feel about all this in a couple of weeks, but that's how I feel right now."

I was sick of it, just sick of it. Sick of the turmoil. He said we'd be working together, but I knew that if we weren't living together, Linwood wouldn't want to work with me, so the contract would be broken and God would have His way.

I asked Pastor Bernard to recommend a divorce lawyer. I went to the lawyer and told him about the divorce, but I also showed him the management contract. He said the same thing the other lawyer did—it was ironclad. But he said, "Perhaps if you offer him something more than what he's getting in this contract, you can tear up this contract and substitute it with another one." He wasn't a music lawyer, and it was stupid of me to have talked to him about it. Pastor Bernard had sent me to him for the divorce, but he had the idea of going to the judge and saying that the only reason I had signed the contract originally was that he was my husband, and that it was part and parcel of the marriage. Now that the marriage was over, the contract was over. Perhaps they'd go for that. If not, then, because of my name, I could get other artists to sign up with us to form a management company. Linwood would still be head of the management company, but I could assign someone else to attend to my own particular needs.

At first I thought this was great, because then he would

not only be getting a percentage of what I made, he'd also be getting a percentage of all these other artists. And he'd be busy, and earning money, so it would not be like I was giving him anything or taking anything from him. Then I thought, if we did that, Linwood would want to manage secular artists, not gospel singers, and my name would be attached to un-Christian-like things they might record. I didn't want that. So we were talking it all back and forth.

A couple of weeks later, Linwood came to me and said he didn't want a divorce. I said, "What?" He said, "Do you know why I asked you for a divorce? It was because I thought you were taking birth control pills."

From early in 1990 I had been getting really heavy duty pains in my back, and found that once again I had fibroids. I'd already had fibroids removed in 1975. Now they were getting worse and worse, and every doctor I went to told me that I would have to have a hysterectomy. But I didn't want that, not only because I was still hoping to have children one day, even at my age, but also because I do believe that if your womb and ovaries were no longer of any use once you were past child-bearing age, God would have made them so they would shrivel up. Well, He didn't, and I wanted to keep everything that God had given me.

I went on refusing the operation for some time, even though every doctor said the same thing. But finally the back pains got worse and worse, and I gave in. I said to the Lord "I know You'll do something. I've been praying to You about not wanting a hysterectomy, but everyone says I've got to do it, so I'm going to schedule it, but I'm still trusting You're going to intervene."

241

I told my friend Carol Williams that I was very reluctantly going to have the operation, and she said she had a book she wanted me to read, *The Castrated Woman*, which she had earlier felt compelled to buy for no apparent reason. In spite of the title, I somehow assumed it was going to make me feel more comfortable about having a hysterectomy. But in a way, I was already reasonably comfortable with the idea, if God was going to let me have it, so I put the book to one side, thinking I'd get around to it later.

I went to see the surgeon and he said my blood count was too low, that I should go away for a month and take iron tablets, and then come back for the operation. I had to go to Italy to make a recording, so I took the book with me, and whenever I had a free moment I read it. In retrospect, I can just hear the Lord saying, "You've been praying for help—read the book, stupid!"

I was sitting in the studio one day, and I got to the end of the book, and I saw a section about a woman gynecologist who had written a book called *No More Hysterectomies*. She believed that fibroids are never a reason for having a hysterectomy.

I put the book down and telephoned Linwood and asked him to find this woman. So he found her. Her name was Dr. Hufnagle. I called her and told her the whole story, and she said, "Don't worry, honey, we'll take care of you." I made an appointment to go and see her out in Beverly Hills, CA.

I then got my secretary, Linwood's sister Denice, to call the surgeon who was going to perform the hysterectomy to say that I was going to get a second opinion and that I'd get back to him, but before she could finish telling him, he slammed the telephone down on her. He was extraordinarily angry. So, I thought, I truly don't want you as my doctor.

I went to Dr. Hufnagle, who examined me and told me she could take care of it without having to remove my plumbing. I went in and she removed more than twenty-one fibroids, in a mass the size of a seven-month-old fetus.

I really don't understand why so many women agree to have hysterectomies. No way would a man have that. A man equates his manhood with his reproductive system. Linwood thought that now my feminine parts were all back together, that I must be having an affair. He'd seen these tiny little iron pills I was taking and he assumed they were birth control pills. Don't ask me why. He'd asked some stupid male friend of his, who'd said, "Yep. That's what they are—birth control pills." They were *iron* tablets. So when he later found out that they were *not* birth control pills, he was satisfied and no longer wanted a divorce.

I'm so insecure, and, well, yeah, I loved him. I've always loved him. But I didn't even have the nerve to say, "Oh, you're just on again, off again. I'm supposed to hop into the marriage and out of the marriage when you snap your fingers, whenever you say, and I have nothing to say about it." That's what I was thinking, and feeling, but I didn't say that. I just said, "All right, Okay."

So I went back to the lawyer and told him that I no longer wanted a divorce, but I allowed him to keep on thinking about his new contract idea. When Linwood found out, he was livid. Positively livid. So I kept trying to come up with ways of arranging this new contract, but without letting Linwood down. It wasn't working out. It had come to a kind of stalemate.

Everything I came up with was not good enough, there was nothing Linwood would accept. And there was no way out of the old contract.

I kept getting bills, because every time you say good morning to lawyers, they charge you for it, but we weren't coming to any conclusions and nothing was happening, except I was paying the lawyer. So I stopped going to him. I wanted the marriage to work, but this thing still came between us, because Linwood knew about it. He went out one night and he stayed away for three nights. I thought, "That's it. Forget it. If he's going to do this, I'm alone anyway. So why bother?" Then I remembered what Pastor Bernard had said about it being a test, and that it was up to me to say something.

I said, "I don't know if this will mean anything to you. A friend of ours once said, 'A warning is a blessing—a gift.' This relationship, this marriage, can very easily deteriorate back to what it was in 1989 if you insist on staying out all night. That's my warning to you." And I got up and walked away. The next morning he said, "You know, I've thought about what you said," and I said, "Good." And nothing else was ever said about it. He's never stayed out again all night, except to stay at his mother's, or with his brother, and then he'll always call me to let me know where he is.

I never believed I was going to divorce Linwood. Even when he asked me for a divorce, I thought, "Well, maybe we will go through with a divorce, but divorced people get remarried all the time." So for me it was only ever going to be on paper. It was never going to be in our hearts.

I think we both felt the same way about marriage and commitment. When we married we became committed to each other for life. We both did, and we both knew we both did. This was just something we had to go through. Once it was over, things would be fine. We were in the dark groping for each other, not knowing how to find our way. It was like, "I smell you. I feel you. But I don't see you and I can't get to you. But I know you are there for me. And I'm here."

Changed
28

*I*t was Pastor Bernard who gave us the first direction. Sometime in 1992 I went for counseling with him on my own. I was still in turmoil. He said, "I hear the Lord telling me to tell you to find, learn, and prepare to minister to the congregation a song called 'Changed.'"

It's a very simple song:

> *A change has come over me*
> *He saved my life and set me free*
> *He washed away all my sins and he made me whole . . .*

I was very interested in the idea, found the song, played it, and . . . I *hated* it! I liked the lyrics, but I hated the melody and the arrangement—I just hated the whole way the song was done. At church the band and the choir all knew and loved the song. The choir would have to sing the song with me, and after the first two very short verses, it was as much the choir as me singing. This didn't bother me, but I just didn't *like* it. Also, in order to be effective, it called for somebody with a really high range. I have had cysts on my vocal cords removed, and ever since then, my range has never been the same—so I wasn't able to perform it as I wanted to.

But God is so clever. He knew I wasn't going to like this song, which meant that I could not "perform" the song. I would have to *minister* the song, because the difference between performing and ministering is that performing is mostly aimed at physical pleasure while ministry is aimed at spiritual edification that glorifies God.

I had not been walking in the changes that the Lord had made in me, because I was afraid to. But perfect love casts out fear. Christ should bring confidence into your life, be your sufficiency. I knew these things, but it was not evident. I knew that if I wasn't walking in them myself, there was no way I was going to be able to minister the song to anyone else. When I understood this, that's when I really began to change and grow.

I began to become confident about myself. I realized the changes really had been made. All I had to do was act like I knew God had wiped away the loneliness. So why was I acting so insecure? When I was away from Linwood I had had no problem being alone. I was fine. Loneliness was gone, so where was the insecurity coming from? It was all part of the lie that the enemy had sold me as a child, and I was still walking in that, instead of walking in the truth of who I had become in Christ.

I began to recognize that I had every reason to be confident. As a matter of fact, I *was* confident. And if Linwood was going to leave me—did it matter? Of course, I loved him. Of course, I wanted him. But I didn't *need* him anymore. I wasn't desperate. So I began to walk in truth. And do you know what happened? Linwood's respect for me began to grow—so much that even I could not believe it. He saw again the girl he had first fallen in love with, who was successful, self-sufficient, and confident, who had a lot going for her.

Because of my desperate need of him in the past, his respect level had dropped, and that's why he had begun to do all the things he had done. I had let myself be treated like a doormat. I had never understood it before. Before I found the Lord, I had had no confidence in anything or anyone. But there was no reason for any of that anymore.

In the past two or three years, as I've changed and grown and been able to grasp and implement in my life more and more the principles and precepts that the Bible teaches, Linwood has been gaining more and more confidence in me, more respect for me, more love for me. What God wanted has come about. Now, in truth, Linwood is not managing me. I am under new management—God is managing me, through Linwood.

*M*alcolm Feld, my agent in England, asked me one day if I thought I'd changed since becoming a Christian, and I said, "Yes."

He said "Well, let me tell you that you have changed very much. In fact, you've made a hundred-eighty-degree turnaround. Before you were a Christian, you were sarcastic, selfish, self-centered, demanding, and thoughtless. But now Gina and I both love you. We love being around you and having you in our home. You are thoughtful, generous, kind, and there's nothing that we wouldn't do for you."

I said, "Malcolm, I must admit, it's not me, but Christ in

me. It's what He has done for me. Only Christ can change the heart of an individual."

And Malcolm said, "Well, I want to tell you—He's doing a great job!"

*M*inistering the song "Changed" made me see a lot of things differently. It confirmed what the Lord told me when He released me to go back to my career in 1990: "As long as your music is created and performed for My glory, and is in keeping with the holy life that I call you to live and advocate, your music is not secular—it is sanctified." I have realized that changing my career to do only gospel music was not what the Lord was calling me to do. I am still to stay in the world I've grown up in, meet people where they are, continue singing the secular music they love, interspersing it with gospel music that is my own style of gospel music—fast, rhythmic gospel music, and meaningful ballads.

That's my directive for now. Whether the Lord will call me to do only gospel music one day, I don't know. Only time will tell. So Sunday by Sunday I go along to church and sing with the choir, and when I feel it's acceptable I sing a few gospel songs in my shows, and for now, that is my ministry. I still hope and believe that one day the Lord will tell me my time has come, and I will bring a full Christian music ministry to a world that was opened up to me by the song "I Will Survive."

Diamond Is a Girl's Best Friend

29

*M*ost people have many acquaintances and very few real friends in life, and I've never been any different, except that I've been blessed since becoming a Christian with four *best* friends. I'm not sure if geography has anything to do with it, but they live nearly three thousand miles apart, from Los Angeles to New York to England.

The one I've known longest is Florence Dixon, nicknamed Fippy, who lives in Los Angeles. I had originally met her in New York, and after she moved away to Los Angeles, we became reacquainted in 1975 when I went out to L.A. to appear on "American Bandstand," to perform "Never Can Say Goodbye." Fippy was already a born-again Christian, the only one I knew at that time. Sometimes Fippy has been the only person in the world I've felt I could confide in.

Sondra, my next best friend, is also my sister-in-law, Sondra Simon Robinson, once of Simon Said. She lives in New York. She's been sister, friend, companion, pal, and mutual confidante, like Fippy, and also roommate, traveling companion, and, of course, backing singer. We've seen much of the world together, and been through innumerable happy and sad experiences, as friends, as professional colleagues, and as members of the same family. And the greatest thing we now share is Christ, because now Sondra, too, has been born again.

My third best friend is Darcel Moreno. I don't mean she's "third best," I just mean—well, you know what I mean. Darcel lives very near us in New Jersey, and I met her at our nearby Gospel Tabernacle Church. Although Darcel is quite a bit younger than I am, she is a very mature Christian, and therefore, through the wisdom of God, we often reverse back and forth the roles of mother and daughter. In giving me motherly advice, Darcel is sometimes passing on the wisdom of her own mother, and there's one saying of her mother's that I've taken very much to heart in preparing this book: Before speaking about someone to anybody else, ask yourself three questions—Is it true? Is it kind? Is it necessary?

That all sounds a bit solemn. Believe me, when Darcel is around, neither of us ever stops talking and laughing. We're the kind of friends who will talk on the phone for an hour, then decide to hang up and visit each other.

I've already mentioned Bebe Russell, whom I met in England in 1988, and she has become my fourth very best friend. I frequently stay with her and her family, when I'm in England, and she was a great support to me when Linwood and I were apart. As time has gone on, our friendship has grown and grown. I've spent many happy hours in their home, and sometimes Linwood, who is also loved by them all now, especially by Bebe's children, comes along too.

I have one other little friend, and this book wouldn't be complete unless I mentioned him. Linwood brought Diamond home as a present for me about four years ago. He was just a little ball of white fluff, small enough to sit in a cereal bowl. I always used to think little dogs, shih tzus, toy poodles, and all little tiny dogs, were useless. I always liked dogs, but I liked big ones, German shepherds, Great Danes, a dog that could protect you and scare someone, not beat you to the hiding place at the first loud noise. And I never liked any dog well enough to let him lick my face or anything like that.

From the moment I picked Diamond up and he started to lick enthusiastically under my chin, all round my neck, I fell instantly in love with him. I thought he was just the sweetest little thing, more like a baby than a dog. I've been in love with him ever since, and everyone who meets him is in love with him. People call me on the phone and say "I met your Diamond, he's just adorable.

I think it's humiliating to stand with a dog on a leash while he does his business, so when I take Diamond for a walk, I take him to the park, find a secluded spot and keep him on the leash until he goes to the bathroom in the proper place. Then I let him run free to play for about twenty minutes. He knows the park now. If he's in the car and we go anywhere near the park, he goes frantic running backward and forward, saying, 'What are you doing? We're in the park! Stop and let me out!" He loves the cold, especially when there's snow. You see this little ball of white wool disappearing into the heaps of snow. He sleeps out on the back terrace when the weather's nice, or in the guest bedroom when it's cold. Linwood had brought him home in one of those dog traveling cages, and at first he would put him in that at night, and put a towel over it. I used to say, "Linwood, he's not a bird."

Then we had a terrible scare. I always went to get him

first thing in the morning. I used to say, "Hi, Diamond!" before I uncovered him, and he would start jumping around, making the cage shake. I'd undo it, and he would leap out and start jumping up and down to greet me, and then run to the terrace door to be let out for his water and food. This particular morning I came in and I said, "Hi, Diamond!" and there was no noise. I thought he was still asleep. I took the cover off, and it was horrible. He was lying unconscious, completely covered in his own excrement. I couldn't bear to even look at him. I woke Linwood up and said, "Something has happened to Diamond. Come and see, come and see."

Linwood said, "Oh no God! Call the doctor." So I called the vet, Dr. Rich, and he said, "Bring him in right away." Linwood took a big towel and wrapped him in it, and carried him down to the car. We didn't know if Diamond was alive or dead. He was completely limp.

Both of us were crying. I knew at that moment that Linwood really loved that little dog. He's normally a very squeamish man, things make him feel sick very easily, but now he was holding Diamond in his arms like a baby. I drove while Linwood held him on his lap, and we were both crying so much I could hardly see. The doctor was only five minutes away. We took him in and the vet cleaned him up and then he took a needle and injected him with fluids.

At first Diamond didn't even open his eyes, but after a while he was trying to raise his head. The vet was very good with us too, because we were beside ourselves. He said, "Don't worry. I'll take care of him. I'll need to keep him for a week."

We had to go away on tour the next day, but by the time we got back Diamond was jumping around, scratching at his cage to get out, and he very nearly did a somersault as soon as he saw Linwood. The vet said, "I thought he was dead, or soon would be, when you brought him in. It was a matter of minutes. But you got him here just in time." I don't know exactly what had happened, but we never put him to bed locked up in his cage again.

Linwood is besotted with Diamond and talks to him like a little person. Someone gave me a stuffed animal, a white fluffy dog when I was in the hospital, and I brought it home. I heard Linwood reprimanding Diamond, who had become amorously attached to it, "No! No! This isn't your wife! Leave it alone!" When he gets irritated, say if you don't let him sit on your lap, he sits and argues with you. You find yourself arguing with this small animal. And he begs. He never gets anything from the table, but hope springs eternal. He sits up looking at you with his big eyes and an expression of such sorrow, as though he's never been fed in his life. He's spent his entire life starving and now he's hoping someone would just give him a scrap.

Diamond is very territorial about out feet, shoes, and socks. The only thing he ever chews is socks. He likes to sit on our feet when we're watching TV. One Christmas somebody gave me a pair of bedroom slippers with little dog faces, and Diamond nearly went mad snapping and barking at these little rivals on my feet.

Unfortunately we aren't allowed pets in our apartment building. People do have them, but someone complained about Diamond being on the terrace, and we got a letter. We don't like to make trouble, so for now he's living with Linwood's mother. He's taken over Linwood's mother's house. Diamond sleeps wherever he wants—the attic, the basement, the bedrooms. He's just taken over the whole place. He's been there now for six months, and really it's a better life for him, with people there all the time and children to take him for walks. So it's enough for him to come and visit us sometimes. He never forgets. Linwood's mother lives in Queens, and we live in New Jersey, and as soon as he sees the George Washington Bridge, he knows he's going home. He gets frantic, and the closer we get to home, the more frantic he gets. As soon as I let him out of the car, he runs straight inside and up the stairs, then down the hall to our door. He scratches until I catch up with him. And then as soon as he's through the door, he makes straight for the two places he knows Linwood will be. Linwood is almost in tears each time Diamond runs and jumps in his lap and licks him all over. It's a precious sight to see.

But he's better where he is, with children to walk him and a yard he can run in. With us he doesn't get out nearly as much as he wants, and after a couple of days he starts running around and around in circles like a maniac. You think there must be two of him, he goes so fast.

What my friends Fippy, Sondra, Darcel, and Bebe all have in common is that they are very loving, caring people. They all have children, whom I love dearly. They all have a personal relationship with the Lord Jesus, as I do. They all love me, and I love all of them. They are as much "family" to me as the children my mother bore. We've laughed, cried, and prayed together. We've experienced and shared so much with each other that time and distance cannot separate us, and because we all have Christ, death won't either.

Irma
30

*L*inwood and I were on tour in Brazil in November 1995. We got back to the hotel one day and they told me that someone had called to say that my sister Irma had been in an accident and was in the hospital. I assumed it was a car accident and that maybe she had broken her leg. Then I thought that it must be quite serious for them to call me in Brazil, so I called back and got through to a member of her husband's family, who told me she was unconscious. They still didn't tell me exactly what had happened, so I wasn't too alarmed. I just thought "unconscious" meant something very temporary and that in a few hours she would be okay. It didn't register with me that she was in a coma. I only had two more days in Brazil performing before we were going home, so that's what we did. I didn't rush back.

When I got home I found that Irma was in a coma, and it hadn't been an accident at all. I'll never know for certain exactly what happened, but this is the story I've managed to piece together from different things people have told me.

On Thanksgiving day Irma had been going to a store, and

on the way she met a girl she knew. They were walking along together chatting when this big young fellow, about eighteen years old, came up to them and started to push the other girl-friend around, shouting at her about some drugs he said she had stolen. He hit her. Irma said, "What do you think you're doing? You don't hit a woman." He said, "Do you want some too?" and went for her, so she started running. He chased her and caught her and hit her, and knocked her to the ground, where he stomped her. He was wearing work boots and he stomped her head. The other girl had disappeared. No one tried to intervene. After the man ran away, a woman came out of her house, recognized Irma, and called for an ambulance. Meanwhile another kid who saw Irma on the ground also knew her, so he ran back to her house, where he found her husband's niece, Anne, who lived on the second floor, and got her to come. By the time the first woman came back out of the house from calling the ambulance, Anne had gotten there and was trying to revive Irma, who was lying on the pavement uncon-scious. But she couldn't wake her up, and then the paramedics came and took Irma away.

By the time I got to the hospital, four days later, she was on a life-support system. I had been told she was unrecogniz-able, but actually she looked pretty good when I first saw her, because they said that she looked so much worse earlier. Her head was still a bit swollen, but her face was normal now. She looked as though she'd had surgery on her head, but she didn't look terrible at all. She was very skinny, but she always had been. She didn't look as though she was experiencing any an-ger or pain or anything. They told me that earlier she had been fighting and they had had to tie her hands down. I suppose in her mind she had never left that scene, so every time she started to gain the slightest bit of consciousness, she was still fighting this guy.

She wasn't tied down when I arrived. She seemed peacefully asleep. I went there every day for a week. I wrote a letter to her and recorded it on tape with gospel music behind my voice, telling her how much she was loved and how her children needed her, and how God loved her, and she had to come out of this because we all needed and loved her so. I would talk to her for a while or read the Bible, then I'd play the tape, because it's hard to keep talking to someone who isn't responding. Then I'd play some soothing gospel music. When I went home in the evening I'd leave the tapes, and the nurses would play them for her when there was no one else there.

When tragedy hits, I deal with it sort of on automatic pilot, and that's exactly the way I was with Irma. I did what I needed to do. There was no way she was going to die. Just no way. She was in a coma and this boy had done this horrible thing—but I did not want to think about the boy. People asked me, "Don't you want to kill him? Don't you want him caught and beaten half to death himself?" One of my brothers was talking about having somebody go and beat him, and other people were even talking about having him secretly killed. I wasn't feeling anything about that boy. I wasn't concerned with what happened to him. I was concerned only with my sister, and her life. I felt that if I started to think about anyone or anything else, I would let her go.

I was convinced from the time that I heard the whole story, as soon as I got home from Brazil, that she was waiting for me, and that as soon as I walked through the hospital door and took her hand and talked to her for a few minutes, she would slowly but surely come out of that coma. When it didn't happen, I thought that it was just going to take a while. I didn't doubt that it was going to happen. I wrote the letter and made the tape, played it for her, prayed for her every day, utterly convinced she was going to come out of it. I called L.A. to speak to and pray with Fippy as I had done with Bebe, Darcel, and Sondra. After our prayer, Fippy said in such a soothing tone that seemed to calm my spirit and bring me peace, "Gloria, Irma is communing with Jesus. She doesn't want to come back."

On the evening of December 6 the hospital called me to say they didn't know if she'd make it through the night as there was no more activity in her brain. Linwood collapsed on the floor. He wept and howled with grief. We went up to the hospital together, and he hugged her and couldn't stop crying. We stayed for a while, but there was nothing we could do, so we went home. I clung to Fippy's words, because they meant that she was at peace and would never suffer again. I returned very early the next morning, and when I arrived they said she was gone.

I didn't cry at first. It was like when my mother died. I couldn't cry until after the funeral. Again, I didn't really grieve until a couple of weeks later. I was dealing with Linwood and his feelings, I was dealing with Irma's three children and what was going to happen to them. One of them, Linwood Maxwell, is Linwood's godson.

Right up until the day of the funeral, I was fine, I was strong. I thought she had gone to be with the Lord. I knew she wasn't a practicing Christian, but I was convinced, and still am, that that was only because she had no knowledge. When you're born again you are like a baby and have to be taught, but she had not been taught. She always said she had a strong faith in the Lord and that He took care of her, so I am sure she has gone on to be with the Lord. I was at peace with that. I had a lot of memories and thought about her a lot, but I didn't grieve. It didn't hit me until ten days later, when I was on a flight to Geneva just before Christmas.

Irma was always a wild child. She thought I was an unbelievably innocent, naive person. She wasn't at all like me, and we lived in different worlds but she spent lots of weekends with us and, we always spent our birthdays and Christmas together. We would go to a lot of trouble choosing presents for each other. Now Christmas was ten days away, and we were not going to be spending it together. Sitting on the plane, I was thinking that I wasn't going to be doing any Christmas shopping for her in Geneva. I had always loved buying her things, and in spite of our different ways of seeing things, I never stopped thinking of her almost as a daughter. And Irma was a wonderful present giver. She never felt that her gifts had to measure up to Gloria Gaynor "the star." She didn't have much money to spend, but she would always find something I really liked, something that showed she had thought about me. She was one of the few people who understood that about me.

I spent most of the flight to Geneva hiding in the toilet, with tears pouring down my face, and I know it sounds pathetic, but what I was feeling most of all was sorrow that my mother wasn't there to help me through this thing. In a way, probably simply because we were the only girls, Irma was much more of a link to my mother than my brothers were, a link to the one person in the world who I know truly loved me. And now they were both gone.

It's still painful. I wonder if I'll ever stop seeing things and thinking, "I must get that for Irma. She'd like that" or, "I must tell her this or see that film with her," and then I think, "Oh no . . . she's gone."

*S*ince Irma died, two of my brothers have also died, Ronald in March and Ralph in May 1996. Ronald had been ill for some time with an aneurism, and Ralph had trouble with his kidneys. Each time I was on automatic pilot. A part of me just wasn't involved. When we had had Irma's funeral, Ronald had prayed like a minister over her, and we were all amazed at how beautifully he prayed. He had become a very active member of a church, although I never knew. At his funeral, which was in his church, his daughter Veronica did a wonderful epitaph for him, and the minister said he'd never heard a father eulogized so beautifully. She played two popular songs, "Because You Loved Me—I'm Everything I Am Because You Loved Me," and one by Mariah Carey, which says, "I'm sorry I didn't say all I wanted to say to you before you passed away." It was very moving and beautiful. Ralph, although he used to sing in the choir, seemed to have drifted away from church a bit, so we had his service at a funeral home. My family members don't seem to live very long—but people in Linwood's family live forever. I once called his grandfather when he was ninety-three—and he couldn't come to the telephone because he was out in the yard chopping firewood.

I know it's sort of a comforting thought, but I don't think

I can really believe that the ones we love continue to watch over us after they're dead. There are no tears in heaven, and I cannot believe that anyone could bear to be looking down on all that is going on here on earth and not cry. I know that God grieves for us, but I wonder if, once He gets us out of all of this, He would allow us the grief of watching what is still going on. In heaven you are at the point where you are not causing yourself or anyone else any grief, so there is no purpose in it. You can't do anything about it. We feel sometimes the presence of angels, and we attribute that feeling to someone we're more familiar with, like a parent or a friend. What you are feeling is pure and simple love—and that is God—but we think it's our mother or someone we know. But what could she do? I think it's more comforting to know we are talking to God who can and does intervene in human affairs in response to the fervent effectual prayers of his children.

God loves everyone, but we humans have a very funny idea of what love is. I used to have the same idea of God's love that many other have—that if God loves you, there's no way He's going to send you to hell. But now I've come to a different understanding, through reading and studying the Bible, in which He explains that because of His undying, unchanging, unconditional love, for each of us, He has made provision through Christ for everyone to go to Heaven. Christ says "I am the truth and the life eternal in Heaven," God the father says "The choice is yours. I set before you life and death, choose life." He doesn't send anyone to Hell.

I believe that the Lord has given me a number of things to draw my conclusions from, so I am at peace with what I feel

station in L.A. It was called "A Seventies Celebration," and it was great. There was Donna Summer, the Bee Gees, Vicky-Sue Robinson, Thelma Houston, K.C. and the Sunshine Band, and Sister Sledge along with seventies' TV personalities. I especially enjoyed it because we were there the whole day together rehearsing for the cameras. Usually, even if you are doing shows together, performers never actually meet because they allot you your own rehearsal times. Many of us knew each other, because although we'd not worked much together in the seventies, we had all been doing the same kind of music, the same kind of shows. Because this was for TV, we had to be there all day, so we had plenty of time to catch up with one another's news. Sister Sledge are Christians now. Donna Summer is a Christian. Thelma Houston is performing all over the world, rather like me, and I've often run into the Village People in Europe.

A year later I did another big revival at the Paramount Theater in Madison Square Garden, with more or less the same artists, and also the Hughes Corporation, the Village People, and Deney Terrio. That was broadcast on radio. I liked that because it was a good show for me to invite some of my Christian friends to, who had never seen me perform. Not many Christians come to see me performing in clubs late on a Saturday night.

Then I did a series of three seventies revival shows on August 9, 10, and 11, 1996, in New Jersey, New York, and Connecticut, which included Kool & the Gang and the Tramps, as well as many other artists who had been in the earlier shows. Deney Terrio was the announcer, and when he was introducing me he said, "Now here is the Real Deal!" Linwood loved that. I also felt complimented when Linwood said he heard one of the performers backstage saying, "Well, thank God for Gloria Gaynor—she's keeping all of us afloat." I thought, "Well, thank God for 'I Will Survive,' 'Never Can Say Goodbye,' and 'I Am What I Am,' because as far as the seventies are concerned, those three great songs have kept me going."

One of the changes that came about in the seventies, of course, was the advent of discotheques, with disc jockeys in the clubs playing records. But also, even during live performances, recorded music began increasingly to take the place of musicians behind the singers. One reason why disco became so popular was that it afforded an inexpensive way of having all the music you wanted without all the expense of bringing in bands.

Musicians got fewer and fewer engagements. Artists began to travel first of all with reel-to-reel tapes, then with cassettes, which were easier but not always reliable, and then finally with digital audiotapes, DATs. It was easier traveling like that, without having to worry about the cost of hotels for up to a dozen people. The ones who suffered were first of all the musicians, of course, but also the audiences. They got to see an artist and hear the music exactly the same as the recording they already knew and loved, but now they were being deprived of the spontaneous creativity that happens between musicians and singers working together onstage.

The singers had mixed emotions about it too. You always had to do the songs in exactly the same way. You couldn't cut off if you wanted to, or make a song longer if it was really going well and the audience was really into it. You could not change the arrangement at all. Some of the new techno music arrangements weren't easily reproduced by live musicians, and then DAT was easier. It was often one person who did all the synthesized techno music, laying track on top of track, so you couldn't have reproduced that sound live. But the overwhelming majority of artists missed having the musicians onstage with them, and the familylike atmosphere, the camaraderie between yourself and the people you worked and traveled with. You began to travel almost alone. You had a tighter space to perform in, too. Sometimes it was virtually just a box to stand on, to make more room for the dancers.

I believe and hope it's beginning to pick up again, as more and more artists—which definitely includes me—want to have the bands back. I do work in some clubs that have bands, and I love that.

Soul Survivor

32

*P*eople often remark about how honest I am about myself. My husband thinks I'm too honest. It sometimes makes me wonder what they truly think of me, because there are still some deeper, darker secrets that I would never tell anybody except the Lord. There are things I share with the public, things I'll only share with close friends, things I'll only share with my husband, and some things I'll only share with the Lord. But people still say, "You're very honest about yourself." Well, I always feel that I'm not intelligent enough to make an original mistake; whatever I've done, somebody else will have also done it, so I can't feel it's any big deal to talk about it.

Even the things I don't tell are not because I think they are so terrible, but because they involve other people. Then again, I only tell things that I think might be edifying to someone else. What's glorifying to the Lord is that I can use my experience to help keep someone from making the same mistakes, or show how I managed to survive.

There's no percentage in lying, which I've done enough in

the past, the Lord knows. People saw right through it because the only thing that shone through then was that I was lying. So now, if the thing that shines through is that I'm being truthful and honest, then that's okay.

When it comes to talking about Linwood and me, I've told you some things that don't show either of us in a very good light. Feminists may think I should have, so to speak, "changed that stupid lock, I should have thrown away the key" instead of marrying him, but men will probably read it and think that they'd have gone just the same as Linwood. The point is, we're not the only two people in the world who have been there, and if it helps others to feel less alone, and less unique in their confusion and unhappiness, and to begin to assess themselves as normal human beings capable of overcoming their own faults and problems, no matter what kind of a mess they are in, then that's been my purpose. Without Christ in one's life, "I will survive" is little more than a catch phrase. I believe it is like a seed that has been put into my life and allowed to grow into an experience. As the Bible says, God gives the increase.

I would say that I've had a relatively happy, but quite difficult, life, but that's who I am. I'm not happy with "easygoing." Even when I choose the songs that I sing, I don't look for songs that are really easy to sing. I don't want a song that's out of my range or ability, but I like to know that I am able to put everything I have into whatever I sing. I've always wanted to feel that I've accomplished something, and have had to put effort into the accomplishment. I like challenges. Now that I am a Christian and am becoming a more mature Christian, the challenges are even greater, but whatever they are, I feel sure I will have the victory through Christ.

So, you see, I have survived. And I will survive.

Of course, I have some regrets about the way I've lived my life. I think there was an easier way to get to where I am now, and I wish I had taken it. I'm not going to moan about it—but I wish I had made better choices. I don't believe people who say they have no regrets. I believe there's always an easier way to get to where you end up as an adult.

I don't think that you really have to trudge through the mud. You know what I'm saying? There's always an easier way to get to where you are, but if you've gone through the worst way, you can sometimes use that to keep someone else from doing the same. Then your mistakes will have served a purpose. Even if I didn't learn by my mistakes, I hope somebody does.

If any young person is reading this book who is lonely and unsure of themselves, as I was, I would say this:

> Find yourself a good Bible teaching church and get some good, clean friends. Finding the church that is right for you isn't always easy, as I discovered, but keep persevering, trying to let God lead you. Being "in" is not all it's cracked up to be, and if you want to grow, and learn about yourself, and discover what it takes to make you who you want to be, then you don't want to follow the crowd, tagging along with wild young people who have had no experience of life. They may be your friends, but don't copy them. You need to learn from the example of people who have been there. You need to read and study the Bible and learn of God so that only He who made you

can tell you who and what you are and your purpose and potential, so others don't limit you.

I would say to all parents:

Your children need to be encouraged, not scolded and criticized. They need to be given a sense of self-worth, and they need to know they are accepted for who they are, not who you think they ought to be. They need to be trusted, praised, appreciated, and given choices, and helped to make the right choices not by words, but by good example.

Parents need to be heroes to their children, and to show them the love of God. If the parents don't give them love and attention, their children will spend the rest of their lives trying to please them. Even after their parents are dead, they'll still be trying to please them instead of God. Children need rules and absolutes, but they need to be able to trust that parents are setting rules and absolutes because they love the children and want what's best for them, not just what's convenient for parents.

I don't really grieve anymore that Linwood and I don't have children, but I feel a loss. I longed to have children, and to show my mother what a great mother I would be. I don't think that Linwood was ever really bothered about it. We've got forty nephews and nieces last time I counted, so I've never been short of children to give affection to.

Linwood still has his publishing company with a couple of writers under contract. I'm still under contract to him as a writer. I'm only writing gospel songs these days, and one day very soon I hope to record an all-gospel album. It will be in the Lord's time.

Linwood is one of those naturally attractive people whom others are always drawn to, especially kids. He's very much a homebody now. He loves his home, and we get along just fine. When I met Linwood, I was looking for a man who was domineering, smart. I wanted him to be guide, guard, and governor of my life. Which is what a father ought to be, and what a husband ought to be. The problem is that neither can do his job properly unless the ultimate guide, guard, and governor in his own life is Christ.

In addition to all the help and blessing I've received from my own church and Pastor Bernard, whenever I'm in L.A. staying with my best friend, Fippy, I go to the Shabach Christian Fellowship, where there is a wonderful minister, Pastor Johnson, who has ministered to me and helped me through many problems. I've been to her church many, many times, and she is a gifted and anointed minister. She had a houseguest called Margaret, who is a lawyer. I will never forget what Margaret said to me when we met, and I have repeated this to many other women, who have been blessed by it. She said, "You know, Gloria, you need to stop relying on your husband to do things for you that he isn't capable of doing. It isn't that he doesn't love you, it's just that there are certain things that he's incapable of doing, and you need to learn that your dependency, and sufficiency, should only be in Christ."

That has relieved me from putting too much pressure on Linwood. It has eased up the tension in our relationship. Linwood recognizes that as his wife, I am representative of the man he is. He taught me, groomed me, appreciated me. He encourages me, protects me, leads me, guides me, and loves me, and is doing a great job. God blesses me with and through Linwood. I was never really satisfied with the way we got married, though, and we will have to renew our vows one day. And I say we'll do it when Linwood is born again, and we'll have a new creation marriage.

For a few years I had my time in the wilderness. In order to grow spiritually, I needed to spend some time away from my professional career, which made things difficult financially. But it was absolutely necessary. Things are better now, and I have no anxiety about the future. Linwood's going to be saved, and it's going to be wonderful. I'm not expecting things to be perfect, but there will be easier communication. It's already much easier when I try to communicate spiritual things to him.

It's funny, because one night when I was praying about Linwood's salvation, about how Linwood felt about me and my "religion," the Lord said, "You're bringing to him the light. It's like when you wake someone up out of the dark, out of a deep sleep. You turn on the light, and the light is very harsh and very irritating, and he gets very cross about it. But after a while he gets used to the light, and then he likes having the light on. And that's what will happen in your relationship."

And that is what is happening. Linwood has already started to share some Christian things with me. For instance, we "adopted" two children as part of a UNICEF program that I wanted to join. He even comes to church with me sometimes, and he thinks Pastor Bernard is wonderful.

He's now gotten to the point that he believes me when I tell him things that have happened in my life, little miracles and things that the Lord has given me, and he's now able to accept those things. He's gotten kind of used to the light. He hasn't completely accepted it for himself yet, but he's grown used to it in my life.

When I wanted to rerecord "I Will Survive" for the *Gloria Gaynor '90* album that I recorded in Italy, which eventually went gold, I wanted to change some of the words to reflect my new Christian beliefs. I wanted to call Freddy Perren's office to ask them if I could do that, because you have to have permission. So I was praying, "Lord, please give me favor with these people. I really don't want to go through any changes with them." I'd had a little difficulty with them in the past, when they had seemed to me to be quite unsympathetic and difficult to deal with.

Linwood didn't want to call them, so I said I would. When we were in the studio in Italy, getting ready to do it, I was trusting God to work it out for me, and Linwood got Freddy Perren's office in Los Angeles on the telephone. He called, "Gloria, do you want to speak to them?" I came over and said, "Hi, Christine! How you doing?"

"Hi, Gloria! Freddy's on the other line. I understand that you want to change some of the words to 'I Will Survive.'"

"Yes, I do. I hope that's not a problem for you." I told her the change I wanted to make.

She said, "Oh, honey! When we heard that you were born again, we were so excited! Praise the Lord! Glory to God!"

They were born again too!